MAY   2012

The Collapse
of the
Soviet Union

MILESTONES
IN MODERN WORLD HISTORY

The Bolshevik Revolution

The Chinese Cultural
Revolution

The Collapse of
the Soviet Union

D-Day and the Liberation
of France

The End of Apartheid
in South Africa

The Iranian Revolution

The Treaty of Versailles

The Universal Declaration
of Human Rights

The Collapse of the Soviet Union

SUSAN MUADDI DARRAJ

CHELSEA HOUSE
PUBLISHERS
An imprint of Infobase Publishing

The Collapse of the Soviet Union

Chelsea House
An imprint of Infobase Publishing
132 West 31st Street
New York, NY 10001

Library of Congress Cataloging-in-Publication Data

Darraj, Susan Muaddi.
The collapse of the Soviet Union / Susan Muaddi Darraj.
  p. cm. — (Milestones in modern world history)
Includes bibliographical references and index.
ISBN 978-1-60413-493-3 (hardcover : alk. paper)
1. Soviet Union—Politics and government—1985–1991—Juvenile literature.
2. Communism—Soviet Union—History—Juvenile literature. 3. Soviet Union—History—Juvenile literature. 4. Soviet Union—Biography—Juvenile literature. I. Title.
DK288.D37 2009
947.085'4—dc22   2008054808

Chelsea House books are available at special discounts when purchased in bulk quantities for businesses, associations, institutions, or sales promotions. Please call our Special Sales Department in New York at (212) 967-8800 or (800) 322-8755.

You can find Chelsea House on the World Wide Web at http://www.chelseahouse.com.

Text design by Erik Lindstrom
Cover design by Alicia Post
Composition by Keith Trego
Cover printed by Yurchak Printing, Landisville, Pa.
Book printed and bound by Yurchak Printing, Landisville, Pa.
Printed in the United States of America

This book is printed on acid-free paper.

All links and Web addresses were checked and verified to be correct at the time of publication. Because of the dynamic nature of the Web, some addresses and links may have changed since publication and may no longer be valid.

CONTENTS

A Public
Challenge

On June 12, 1987, Ronald Reagan, the president of the United States, made his second visit to West Berlin—the divided capital of the long-divided German nation.

Reagan, a tall, charismatic leader, stood before the Brandenburg Gate near the Berlin Wall, the structure that had been erected by Soviet troops, who had controlled and policed East Germany (and East Berlin) since the end of World War II. After the war's end in 1945, the nation of Germany was divided into two separate countries: the Federal Republic of Germany, also known as West Germany (as well as West Berlin itself, which was well within the Soviet zone), and the German Democratic Republic, also known as East Germany, which included East Berlin, both formed in 1949.

U.S. President Ronald Reagan speaks before the Brandenburg Gate, near the Berlin Wall, on June 12, 1987. During the speech, Reagan called on Soviet President Mikhail Gorbachev to "tear down this wall." Pictured with Reagan are West German Chancellor Helmut Kohl *(right)* and President of the German Parliament Philipp Jenninger *(left)*.

East Germany, with a Communist government, fell under the Soviet sphere of influence, while West Germany had a democratic government. The Berlin Wall was built in 1961 to prevent East Berliners from fleeing to West Berlin; many escaped to the other side (or died in the attempt) as the negative aspects of Soviet rule became apparent. In fact, by the time of President Reagan's visit in 1987, the contrast between East Berlin and West Berlin was striking: economically, socially, and politically, the western side offered far more freedom and a higher standard of living than its Soviet-influenced counterpart.

In his speech, which was televised throughout West Germany but also heard in East Berlin over the wall, Reagan highlighted this stark contrast: "In the West today, we see a free world that has achieved a level of prosperity and well-being unprecedented in all human history. In the communist world, we see failure, technological backwardness, declining standards of health, even want of the most basic kind—too little food. Even today, the Soviet Union still cannot feed itself."[1]

Then, he issued a challenge to Mikhail Gorbachev, the Soviet leader: "General Secretary Gorbachev, if you seek peace, if you seek prosperity for the Soviet Union and Eastern Europe, if you seek liberalization: Come here to this gate! Mr. Gorbachev, open this gate! Mr. Gorbachev, tear down this wall!"[2] It was a resounding call, one that made headlines around the world. For Reagan, and much of the Western world, the division of Berlin was a symbol of the Cold War, a physical manifestation of the tension that existed between the West and its capitalist system and the East and its Communist regime.

Reagan's comment that the Communist world displayed its failures was a way to remark on the struggles the Soviet Union was experiencing. No one suspected that less than four years later, not only would the Berlin Wall be torn down, but the Soviet Union, and along with it the vast Russian Communist empire in Eastern Europe, would also fall. In fact, Gorbachev would help sow the seeds of its destruction.

THE ROOTS OF THE RUSSIAN EMPIRE

The Union of Soviet Socialist Republics (USSR), which was founded in 1922 following the Bolshevik Revolution of 1917, had a tremendous impact on world history, only one part of which was the erection of the Berlin Wall. To understand the rise of the USSR, it is important to first understand the legacy of the Russian people and the Russian empire. Communism took hold in Russia only because of the long history of class suppression by aristocrats, czars, and emperors over centuries. The USSR would eventually be composed of Russia and several other republics. Russia was by far the largest republic, and the dominant ethnic group was the Russian people. This, however, was not always the case.

As a geographic entity, the region we now call Russia was originally occupied by many different ethnic peoples, such as the Sarmatians, the Goths, the Khazars, and other ancient groups. A major shift occurred in A.D. 862 when the Varangian people—also known as the Rus—established a government in the city of Kiev. According to Derek Maus, editor of *Russia*, they were led by their king, Riurik.[3] The Varangians were seafaring warriors of Swedish origin (the word "Rus" may have its origins in the Nordic words "Ropsmenn" or "Ropskarlar," which mean "men of the rudder," according to Maus).[4] The Rus overcame the other Slavic tribes in the region, although some local leaders actually invited Riurik and his people in to settle internal problems.

While the Rus built Kiev as a powerful city, they did not isolate themselves from the rest of the world. In fact, they interacted with neighboring cultures, which led them to borrow the Cyrillic alphabet and the Orthodox Christian faith from the neighboring Byzantines.[5] Cyrillic, according to Maus, was brought by St. Cyril, a Byzantine monk; the alphabet was "a combination of Greek, Roman, and other characters that allowed the religious writings of the Orthodox Church to be translated from Greek into Old Russian, thereby greatly facilitating the spread of Christianity among the predominantly Slavic populace of the Kievan state."[6]

Kiev, with the Rus strength and the Byzantine influences in terms of language and religion, grew in power, but it was no match for the Mongols who arrived in 1238, led by Genghis Khan. The Mongols defeated the Rus and ruled from 1238 until 1480, a period of almost 250 years known as the "Mongol Yoke," according to Leo de Hartog.[7] During the Mongol period in Russia, many aspects of life changed. For example, the city of Muscovy, later known as Moscow, became the center of the empire, which moved influence away from the city of Kiev. The Mongols, according to de Hartog, established an efficient and beneficial tax system, a courier service, and a strong communication system. Also, the Mongols had a dynastic system of rule known as the Golden Horde, which was a khanate, or the system of government ruled by a khan, or emperor. The khan held absolute power over his subjects and the people in the domain he ruled.

When the Russians eventually overthrew the Mongols, they adopted the Golden Horde model as a political system. Ivan, a prince from Moscow, led an army to oust the Mongols (by 1480, the Mongols had become weaker and more ineffectual, making Ivan's mission slightly easier). He later became known as Ivan III, the first czar of Russia; the term "czar" was adopted from the Roman name "Caesar," which had come to mean emperor or absolute ruler starting in the early years of the Roman Empire. Indeed, Ivan IV, his successor, ruled with absolute authority, crushing the opposition at every opportunity, so much so that history remembers him as Ivan the Terrible. Ivan III, according to historian Jules Koslow, smoothly moved into the role of czar because the stage had been set for him during the Mongol Yoke:

> The two-hundred-odd years of Tatar [Mongol] subjection,
> in which the authoritarian khans had acted with proverbial
> Oriental despotism, had had its influence, penetrating in a

A color woodcut of the first Russian czar, Ivan IV, also known as Ivan the Terrible, who reigned from 1533 to 1584.

subtle way into the very fabric of Russian governmental life and into the very relation of the Russian princes and their subjects. With only a few exceptions . . . there was no democratic tradition, no body of literature, philosophy, or law that concerned itself with the rights of men.[8]

Ivan the Terrible's absolute rule was possible, therefore, because the Russian people had become accustomed to being ruled absolutely. He established an area, compromising half the land of Russia, known as the *Oprichnina*, which he gained by forcing it away from nobles and landowners, whom he considered to be too powerful. The Oprichnina was also an institution that helped guarantee and protect Ivan's power. It represented a large group of fiercely loyal officers who operated as a brutal police force for Ivan: They spied for him and violently suppressed any threats to his power. Interestingly, by stealing land from the nobles and forcing many into exile, Ivan IV won the support of many of Russia's peasantry. According to Koslow, "By waging what can well be termed a 'class war' against the boyars [landowning nobles], Ivan had a propaganda weapon that endeared him to the mass of the Russian people, who hated the selfish, greedy, merciless boyars."[9] Koslow also points out, however, that the nobles would later return to power because they, unlike the mass of illiterate poor Russians, were equipped to govern the country.

While Ivan seemed to support the poor by attacking the rich, he did nothing to improve the lives of the miserable masses. Nonetheless, the issue of "class war"—the battle between the entitled rich, who were the minority, and the impoverished masses, who were the vast majority—had been introduced. It would become a repeating theme in Russian history.

Class Struggle in the Czarist State

Mikhail Fedorovich Romanov, known as Czar Michael, was almost 17 years old when he became Russia's leader in 1613. Although he is not remembered as a very effective czar, his ascension to the throne did establish the Romanov dynasty, which would endure until being overthrown in 1917 by the Bolsheviks, led by Vladimir Lenin.

The Romanov rulers who succeeded Czar Michael put many reforms into place that ironically would lead to the 1917 revolution that transformed Russia into the Soviet Union. The first of these reforming czars was Pyotr Alexeyevich Romanov, who is known as Peter the Great. His lengthy reign lasted from 1682 until 1725, which allowed him 43 years to put his ideas for revitalizing Russia into effect. Above all, Peter wanted to modernize his country. For Peter, who had traveled widely in Europe and been impressed by its modernity, "reform" meant bringing European ways and notions to Russia's culture. In the early 1700s, Europe was entering the Age of Enlightenment, when philosophers and writers advocated reason, rather than faith alone, as the source of authority and key to progress—a revolutionary departure from the concepts of aristocracy, oligarchy, theocracy, and the divine right of kings. The age's key thinkers, philosophers, and writers included luminaries such as Thomas Hobbes, Edmund Burke, John Locke, and Thomas Paine.

Czar Peter's own country was far from the ideals of the Enlightenment. At the time, Russia was and had always been a largely impoverished country in which many of its citizens were serfs—people who lived on and worked the land owned by a lord or a nobleman. Furthermore, these people, their families, and property were owned by their lord, and though they worked the soil, the fruits of their labor belonged to the lord. Serfs were prohibited from moving to other properties, but their lord could sell them if he chose. In practice, serfdom was a form of slavery, although a serf had some form of protection in that the lord could not kill him or injure him (as historians point out, however, this happened nonetheless). While some Russians understood and objected to the system of serfdom, the fact was that the economy of the Russian countryside had depended on it for generations.

Czar Peter saw other problems with any attempt to modernize Russia, namely the high rate of illiteracy and what he saw as a culture that was too traditional and religious. For example, the Russian Orthodox Church played a major role in Russian society and politics, controlling most of the educational sphere and holding great influence over the ruling classes. Despite the Church's influence, Peter the Great set out on a plan to secularize Russia: nonreligious schools were opened and nonreligious books printed. At this time, historian D.S. Mirsky notes, "The

An oil-on-canvas portrait of Czar Peter I, also known as Peter the Great, who modernized Russia during his lengthy reign, which lasted from 1682 to 1725.

Church ceased to be the sole depository of learning." Previously, the literary language of Russia was Church-Slavonic, but it was soon replaced by the Russian language itself, which, in the past, had been deemed not "high" enough.[1]

Peter also ordered his subjects to begin dressing in a more European fashion, commanding military and court officials, as well as most men of the nobility, to shave their beards; those who refused were forced to pay a beard tax. Many Russians benefited from Peter the Great's secular reforms, notably those in the middle classes and the military. These groups also benefited from Peter's industrial reforms, which the reform-ist czar also imported from the Europeans. Mirsky explains that the "essential content [of the Reform] was the adoption of European technique and technical instruction, the encourage-ment of essential industries, the creation of a modern army and navy, and the radical secularization of the body-politic."[2] By boosting the country's industrial base and strengthening its military, Peter helped the military and the rising middle class (particularly business people who owned factories, mines, and other industries) to flourish during this time. These people, most of whom had no connections to the nobility and land-owning class of lords, finally had a chance to accumulate wealth and social status under Peter the Great.

Unfortunately, while certain classes of Russians thrived under Peter's reforms, others, namely the peasant and serf classes, were crushed beneath them. When new factories were established, the owners were given serfs to work in them; the peasant and serf classes were taxed heavily and used to build St. Petersburg, a glorious city built to honor the czar. As Mirsky writes of the lower classes, "All burdens were heaped upon them, with no corresponding advantages."[3] Later in his reign, Peter was crowned Emperor of All Russia, although it is certain that not all Russians benefited from his rule.

As they had throughout Russian history, the poor and working classes of Russia suffered, in contrast to the upper classes. The bitterness implanted in the lower classes by Peter's reign would last and influence future generations of Russians.

CATHERINE AND THE ENLIGHTENMENT

Catherine II, known as Catherine the Great, ruled Russia as its empress from 1762 until her death in 1796. Born Sophie Augusta Fredericka, she was a German-Prussian princess and not ethnically Russian. Her husband Peter III, grandson of Peter the Great, was assassinated a few months into his reign. (Some historians suggest that his politically ambitious wife aided in planning and carrying out the assassination plot.) When she rose to power, Catherine asserted her authority by taking on the title Empress of All the Russias.

In many ways, Catherine was a student of Peter the Great; she admired European culture and traditions and wished to secularize and modernize Russia using Europe as a model. She set about reforming Russia wholly, thus leading historians to call her reign the "Era of Enlightenment for Russia." As historian James H. Billington writes, however, Catherine's Enlightenment would have a "revolutionary nature and fateful consequences."[4]

The Russian Orthodox Church saw its power and influence wane under Peter the Great; under Catherine, that power was further crippled because the empress wholly supported the philosophy of the Enlightenment, especially as practiced by the French. She corresponded with many Enlightenment thinkers and writers—such as Voltaire, the author of *Candide* and other well-known works—who were known to be critical of the Church and countered its teachings of obedience and faith with their own emphasis on individual reason and education.

In accordance with her beliefs and her desire to secularize Russia, Catherine ordered monasteries to be closed in order to lessen the power of the clergy. She viewed the hierarchy of priests, bishops, and other church leaders as a negative force in Russian society, binding Russians and their culture to the past. She wanted to direct Russia to a new future. Furthermore,

Catherine the Great, the Russian empress who expanded the empire, improved its administration, and continued its modernization along Western European lines. During her reign, Russia was recognized as one of the great powers of Europe.

under Catherine, Russian cities were rebuilt and expanded, and made over to be more European in their appearance and design. She encouraged and even ordered museums and galleries to be built, as well as the first public library in Russia, to encourage learning and the arts. Billington adds: "More than any other single person prior to the Leninist revolution, Catherine cut official culture loose from its religious roots, and changed both its physical setting and its philosophical preoccupations." By physical setting, Billington adds, Catherine's formula was essentially to trade "city for monastery."[5]

Her encouragement of the arts and learning helped contribute to the rise of the intelligentsia, defined by Billington as "a new class of secular intellectuals vaguely inclined toward sweeping reform." He adds that the intelligentsia became a rank sandwiched between "the ruling aristocracy and the servile peasantry."[6]

While she encouraged education and targeted the Church, Catherine failed to apply a major tenet of the Enlightenment era in Europe: its insistence on lessening the dominance of the upper class and aristocracy over the impoverished lower classes. Indeed, under Catherine, and Peter before her, the peasant classes and serfs suffered tremendously, producing resentment against the aristocracy. Because class tensions had already been mounting for generations, one of the major domestic political issues Catherine faced during her reign was class-related: the Pugachev uprising. The Cossack Emelian Pugachev, who was a member of one of the militaristic groups that lived in the steppe regions of Ukraine and also southern Russia, led a revolt against Catherine's authority in the fall of 1773. The widely popular revolution spread quickly, and soon major cities were overtaken by its leaders. Pugachev appealed to serfs and the lower classes by promising social justice, and they responded in masses. After he and his followers had conquered substantial territory, Pugachev, at the height of the uprising, declared himself an emperor and set up a parallel court to compete with that of Catherine in St. Petersburg. The uprising, however, was poorly organized, and Pugachev's army was defeated in battle against Catherine's forces. In 1774, Pugachev's own men turned him in to the royal army; he was later executed in Moscow. Despite its failure, the Pugachev uprising remains an important moment in Russian history because it demonstrated how frustrated the lower classes were and how easily the masses could be inspired to revolt.

As Billington explains, Catherine faced another type of rebellion later in her reign: "the first appearance of the 'Pugachevs from the academies,'" which he describes as "a new kind of opposition from within the educated aristocracy."[7] These intellectual Pugachevs resented social injustice and class divisions and strove to seek ways to level the power structure in Russian society.

EMANCIPATION

Catherine, who had championed reform, did little to improve the standing of the serfs; indeed, as it had under Peter, their condition worsened during her 30-plus-year reign. It was not until the ascension of Czar Alexander II to the Russian throne that serfs saw anything legally and officially done on their behalf.

On March 3, 1861, Czar Alexander Nikolayevich II issued an "Emancipation Manifesto," a document that radically changed the Russian economy and society. In this groundbreaking document, Alexander asserted that serfs would become peasants with "new rights," including a section of land on which they could sustain themselves by raising livestock and planting crops, and would have the right to live in their homes in exchange for a "specified obligation," such as a period of labor, they owed their lords. Alexander made it clear in his manifesto that once the obligation to the lord had been fulfilled, the serf could buy his home. At that point, he would no longer be a serf but a "free peasant landowner."[8]

JUSTICE AND HUMAN RIGHTS

For centuries, the serfs and lower classes in Russia had sought freedom and equality. These lower classes were so long ignored by monarchs and even the leaders who claimed to sympathize with their plight, that their struggle helped contribute to the appeal of Communist ideology in early twentieth-century Russia.

For example, during Catherine's reign, when many in society were embracing the tenets of the Enlightenment, which included individual liberty, the poor continued to suffer. In fact, poverty and widespread hunger only grew worse during Catherine's reign as empress. There was some hope of reform in 1767, when Catherine convened the Legislative Commission, a body of elected representatives from each of the classes; however, while peasants were included, serfs were not. Furthermore, the commission failed to address the legality of the serf system.

Many uprisings and revolts, in favor of more freedom and opportunity, took place in Russia. The Pugachev Rebellion had a major impact, but other, smaller revolts also occurred. By the mid-1800s, the serf population averaged about a third of the entire population of Russia, at a time when most of the world had condemned slavery. Serfdom was finally abolished in 1861, but the conditions of the emancipation (enacted by Alexander II) were not favorable. Furthermore, the victory was not a tangible one: After his assassination, living conditions for the freed serfs continued to decline.

The frustration of the lower classes, built up over so many centuries, provided a favorable milieu for the early Marxists and Communists who preached that power should be placed in the hands of the working people.

Alexander knew that his policy would rupture ties between his government and the landowners, who also held much power in Russia, but he pursued it nonetheless. He did allow two years to put these changes into effect, during which time the class system in Russia saw its first major overhaul in centuries, as serfs broke free of the bondage in which they lived under the boyars. In 1881, however, 20 years after issuing his manifesto, Czar Alexander was assassinated by a group that planted several bombers in a crowd while the czar's carriage traveled; the first bomb failed to kill him, but a second bomb, thrown minutes later, succeeded. Some historians, such as W.E. Mosse, argue that while Alexander II had good and humanitarian intentions, he simply was not an effective leader. After his death, the reform movement suffered a major setback.

His successors, Czar Alexander III and Czar Nicholas II, took a much firmer hand in ruling Russia. They both tightened control over the government, centralizing much of it in the hands of the czar himself. However, they—and especially Czar Nicholas—were overly zealous in the ways that they crushed popular rebellion.

In 1905, an uprising exploded in Russia, fueled by a poor economy and a frustrated population tired of the czar's harsh treatment. The uprising blossomed into what is now called the 1905 Russian Revolution, although, as far as revolutions go, it was an unfocused one. Its participants ranged from those who were unhappy with the slow pace of reform, to those who called for democracy and an end to the monarchy, to those who simply were fed up with the treatment of the lower classes. The violence, directed mostly at the government, spread quickly throughout the Russian empire. The revolution took the form of strikes and protests, causing chaos and unrest. After revolutionaries assassinated his uncle, the governor general of Moscow, the czar was forced to act.

Reluctantly, Nicholas II succumbed to the main demand of the revolutionaries, that the population have representation in their government rather than be subjected to the will of one man, the czar. On October 30, 1905, Nicholas II issued what is known as the October Manifesto, which eroded his own power as czar and established a parliament of lawmakers, known as the Duma. The Russian people would elect members of the Duma in regularly held elections. The October Manifesto specifically stated, "No law shall become effective without the confirmation by the State Duma, and that the elected representatives of the people shall be guaranteed an opportunity of real participation in the supervision of the legality of the acts by authorities whom We shall appoint."[9]

Democracy had finally arrived in Russia, albeit in an infant form and against the will of the czar. It would not last long.

The Bolshevik Revolution

The reign of Czar Nicholas II ended in 1917, though he had acceded to all of the demands of his people. By that year, everything had changed in Russia. In addition to plunging the nation deeply into World War I (1914–1918), the czar, as well as the royal family, had fallen into disfavor, due in great part to their association with the mystic Grigori Rasputin, a shadowy figure who was very influential in the lives of the czar and his wife, Czarina Aleksandra. The czarina especially relied on Rasputin, who claimed to be a prophet and a healer, for advice on even the most minute details of her life. A group of nobles, alarmed by the power Rasputin had over the royal family, assassinated him in December 1916. The damage done to the reputation of Czar Nicholas II was tremendous, however, and calls for reform increased. In March 1917, Czar Nicholas II abdicated, or stepped down from, the Russian throne, and a provisional government composed of members of the Duma assumed power in Russia.

In the meantime, many political parties attempted to fill the void left by the removal of Czar Nicholas II and assume leadership of Russia. The Communists, who had been organizing in Russia since the late 1800s, were one of these groups. Their philosophy was inspired by *The Communist Manifesto*, a political tract published in 1848 by German philosophers Karl Marx and Friedrich Engels, which argued that a state controlled by the workers would be far more beneficial than any capitalistic society. Marx, who lived from 1818 to 1883, observed the industrial transformation of the European economy taking place, as well as the social injustice that accompanied it. He saw European cities becoming crammed with poor people from the countryside going to work in their factories, where they were frequently exploited by those who owned the businesses and means of industry. As poor people labored and often were maimed and even died in these factories, business owners grew rich. Marx came to view capitalism as an immoral and unjust way to accumulate wealth.

Socialism was intended to fix the divided class system. As William E. Watson notes, "Believing his theories to be the solution to global injustice, [Marx] advocated revolution by the proletariat (industrial working class) against its alleged exploiters, the bourgeoisie (capitalist class). He predicted that a clash between proletariat and bourgeoisie was imminent and unavoidable."[1]

Since the time of Catherine the Great and her Enlightenment reforms, a group of intellectuals had gained strength in Russian society. Many of these intellectuals adopted the ideas laid out in Marx's work, believing that if Russia could successfully adopt socialism, it could help spread the political philosophy to the nations of Europe and North America. They felt that the clash between proletariat and bourgeoisie predicted by Marx would occur first in Russia, and that their country could be the first to successfully implement Marx's ideas and help spread them to other nations.

In 1898, this group of intellectuals, known as "Legal Marxists," met in Minsk and formed the Russian Social-Democratic Workers' Party (RSDWP). The group adopted a manifesto, which stated: "The Russian proletariat will throw off the yoke of autocracy, and thus with greater energy will continue the struggle against capitalism and the bourgeoisie for the complete victory of socialism."[2]

Communism, however, not socialism, was the end goal of Marx's vision. Socialism was but an intermediate step on the path that would end in an ideal society in which the proletariat, or working class, would determine its own future. Under socialism, the government would control the society's means of production until the proletariat was able to actively serve its own interests. Communism would be the final stage in which both class dichotomies and the state itself ceased to exist. Before that was to happen, however, the illiterate lower classes of Russia, which had been subjugated for hundreds of years by the Mongols to the monarchy, would need to undergo a mass reeducation in order to participate fully in the new order.

Marx's writing influenced generations of Russian intellectuals. He published *Das Kapital*, which argued that capitalism thrived only because it exploited the working classes, without sharing any of the benefits or profits with them. In 1872, the treatise was translated into Russian. It solidified an already forming trend among intellectuals toward adopting socialism as their ideology. Interestingly, Marx himself did not think that a socialist revolution would occur in Russia because he believed, as Richard Sakwa notes, that "preconditions for a proletarian revolt in Russia would not develop for hundreds of years."[3] Russia did not have a large proletarian population, as many European nations did because it was still a mostly agrarian society rather than an urban industrial one. Nevertheless, those Russians who were won over to the socialist cause saw a similar system of oppression in the czarist government, which dominated Russian politics, and in the plight of the serfs and peasant classes.

LENINISM

One Russian who advocated socialism was Vladimir I. Ulyanov, who later came to be known as Vladimir Lenin. He became a fervent follower of Marx's ideas, although many historians agree that Lenin changed many of Marx's tenets to suit the Russian context. For example, Marx believed that, after a socialist revolution, nations would be governed by a "dictatorship of the proletariat," or led by the working classes. Lenin advocated that the nation be ruled by both the proletariat and the peasant class, as the industrial class in Russia was quite small. Also, many Russians who believed in Marxist ideas were members of the bourgeoisie themselves, who opposed the czar and his regime. Satwa noted that Lenin advocated that the revolution would be a highly organized effort, triggered and maintained by a small and close-knit group of these people, some of whom would even receive a salary for their efforts.[4]

Another leader who emerged in the late nineteenth and early twentieth centuries was Leon Trotsky. Born in 1879 in the Ukraine, which was then part of the Russian empire, Trotsky was a revolutionary and political activist who became enamored with Marxist theory and believed that a socialist revolution could happen in Russia. He would eventually help establish and command the Soviet Union's Red Army. One of the socialist movement's intellectual leaders, Trotsky grew powerful within the Russian Communist Party.

In Russia at this time, a system of soviets, or councils, existed, especially in Moscow and in St. Petersburg. They

In this sketch from 1942, four major Communist leaders are pictured from left to right: Karl Marx, Friedrich Engels, Vladimir Lenin, and Joseph Stalin.

helped collect and express in a political manner the opinions and needs of the working classes. Trotsky was pleased by this development, as it made credible his claim that the working class would take care of its own interests. In 1904, one year before the first soviets were established, he had written: "Poorly or well (more poorly) we are revolutionising the masses, arousing in them the simplest political instincts."[5] Trotsky believed that, by triggering these instincts, Communists could help inspire the working class to organize its own efforts on its own behalf. The soviets seemed to make that a reality because they were councils of working-class people organizing to determine what was in the best interests of their own members.

THE BOLSHEVIKS

By the time that Czar Nicholas II stepped down from the throne in February 1917, Russian Communists were poised to step in. Their cause was helped by the fact that the Pro-

VLADIMIR LENIN

Vladimir Ilich Ulyanov, who later renamed himself Vladimir Lenin, was born in 1870 in the Russian city of Simbirsk. His father was the head of the public education system in the region, and was considered a nobleman. The family was a political one; however, tragedy struck when Vladimir's older brother was arrested and killed under suspicion that he had belonged to a group that tried to assassinate the emperor.

Young Vladimir himself would become politically involved and fall into trouble as well. During his first few months at law school, he was expelled for joining a student demonstration. While he eventually completed his law studies, he soon gave up practicing law, preferring to spend his time and efforts in political, revolutionary work. Many Russians had been swept up in the socialist movement, and Lenin was no different. He devoured the work of Karl Marx, especially the influential work *Das Kapital*, and moved to St. Petersburg, then the Russian capital, to become more active in politics.

In the city, Lenin found that the socialist organizations there were busy: according to Orlando Figes, Lenin and others "began working with the industrial workers of the city to increase the workers' awareness of their political and economic power." Lenin's advocacy of the working class landed him in trouble many times, and he spent many of the next several years imprisoned or in exile. In fact, he wrote his first political tome, *The Development of*

visional Government was not successful and that the people were becoming frustrated by its failing efforts to reform Russia, as had been promised. This was due to the fact that the Provisional Government was finding it almost impossible to

Capitalism in Russia, in 1899 while serving a sentence in exile with his wife, also a political activist.

He continued writing over the next few years, arguing that Russia—despite being an agricultural society and seemingly unsuited to Marx's belief that socialist revolution would only work in an industrial society—was still ripe for revolution. He also edited two socialist newspapers, *Iskra* (The Spark) and *Vperyod* (Forward), and established himself as a leading voice within the Russian Social Democratic Labor Party (RSDLP), a political party that made the monarchy nervous and whose members routinely faced arrest and harassment. Nevertheless, the RSDLP was growing stronger, especially when Lenin's faction, the Bolsheviks, assumed a stronger role by arguing that the revolution that would happen in Russia would be propelled by a select group of professionals, who would teach the workers to later take control of their own political futures.

After the Bolshevik Revolution of 1917, Lenin helped the Bolsheviks maintain their grip on power during the Russian Civil War, and ushered the nation into its new phase as the Union of Soviet Socialist Republics, a name it assumed in 1922. Shortly afterward, however, Lenin—who was seen as the father of the socialist movement in Russia—suffered a series of strokes that left him progressively weaker. Before his death in 1924, he warned his colleagues that the USSR should not be ruled by authoritarians such as Joseph Stalin. By then, however, Stalin and his cronies were too powerful. Upon Lenin's death, St. Petersburg, which had been renamed Petrograd, was again renamed Leningrad to honor him, and his body was put on public display in Moscow's Red Square.

put major economic and social reforms into effect while World War I, then known as the Great War, was raging.

The Social Democratic political party in Russia was growing in its appeal and popularity. In the early 1900s, before the abdication of Czar Nicholas II, these socialists had split into two factions: the Bolsheviks and the Mensheviks. The first group, led by Lenin, was in the majority (thus its name, derived from the Russian word "bol'shinstvo," or "majority") and argued for a socialist movement that was tightly controlled until, so they said, their revolution could be assured. The latter group, which was in the minority (from the Russian "menshinstvo," for the same), wanted to keep the movement broad and open to everyone and to allow the socialist fervor to evolve gradually within Russian society.[6] Trotsky supported the Menshevik efforts, but the Bolsheviks, especially Lenin, portrayed the Mensheviks as intellectuals who were not aggressive enough and were afraid to make bold moves.

Lenin's political tract "One Step Forward, Two Steps Backwards" offers a good idea of the Bolsheviks' revolutionary brand of socialism: "One step forward, two steps backwards—It happens in the lives of individuals, and it happens in the history of nations and in the development of parties. . . . In its struggle for power the proletariat has no other weapon but organization. . . . Its ranks will become more and more consolidated, in spite of all zigzags and backwards steps."[7]

Many Russians were attracted to the political ideas of the Bolsheviks. As Geoffrey Hosking writes, "The appeal of the Bolsheviks lay in their programme of 'peace, land and bread.' "[8] Some members of the Bolsheviks wanted to cooperate with the other parties, including the Provisional Government, in order not to jeopardize the current situation following the fall of the czar. Many Russian Communists, however, wanted to pull out of the Great War, something the Provisional Government was not inclined to do. Lenin himself urged this route, but others disagreed, especially when they realized that the Germans sup-

Revolutionaries armed with rifles take aim during the Bolshevik Revolution in October 1917.

ported Lenin, which made the suggestion suspicious because Germany was Russia's enemy in the war and, of course, would benefit from a Russian withdrawal. Indeed, when others learned of the German support, the Bolsheviks' reputation suffered.

Instability continued to loom until August 1917, when General Lavr Kornilov attempted a military coup. Leading a small army, he planned to purge St. Petersburg of the Bolsheviks. His plans, however, were stopped by both the Provisional Government and the Bolsheviks themselves. Indeed, the attempt proved embarrassing for Kornilov, whose troops were ultimately persuaded to join the Bolsheviks and abandoned his cause. Hosking writes, "This fiasco dramatically revived the fortunes of the Bolsheviks," who quickly became the largest political party vying for power. Their militia, the "Red Guards," swelled in numbers and, on October 9, 1917, the Military Revolutionary Committee (MRC) was formed in St Petersburg.[9]

Two weeks later, on October 23, the Provisional Government attempted to arrest many of the Bolshevik leaders and shut down their newspaper offices. Leon Trotsky commanded the MRC to protect the newspapers and maintain order. Lenin saw this moment as the opportunity to finally seize power. He urged the MRC to arrest the members of the Provisional Government. Indeed, he had been calling upon the Bolsheviks to seize power for the past few months. In one letter to the Bolshevik Central Committee, he wrote, "Dear comrades! Events so clearly indicate the task for us that any delay would be tantamount to a crime. . . . The Bolsheviks do not have a right to wait for the congress of soviets, they must take *power immediately*. In this way they will save the world revolution . . . and the Russian revolution."[10]

The Bolshevik leaders finally acceded to Lenin's wishes. The arrests of the Provisional Government's members took place on October 25, and the Bolsheviks were now in full control of the Russian government, in a revolution that was startlingly bloodless and efficient. Hosking notes how the Bolsheviks cemented their popularity among the people: "The Bolsheviks had seized power under the guise of defending the soviets against a Provisional Government bent on undermining them."[11] Those people who supported the Bolsheviks, however, expected that, as Hosking explains, "a coalition socialist government" that drew its authority from the soviets would follow the revolution. This did not happen.

War at Home
and Abroad

U pon seizing control of the Russian government, one of the first actions of the Bolshevik leaders was to pull Russia out of World War I, which would not end until November 1918 with the defeat of Germany and the victory of the Allies (the United States, France, and Great Britain). The withdrawal from the war, however, did not mean that the new Communist leadership of Russia would have peace. Between 1918 and 1920, civil war raged in Russia between the new powers of the Bolsheviks, who were known as the "Reds," and a loose confederation of counterrevolutionary forces known as the "Whites"—mostly conservative Russian army leaders. The Bolsheviks eventually persevered and defeated the challenges to their leadership.

According to Evan Mawdsley, this victory was achieved due to several factors. The Bolsheviks already controlled St.

Petersburg and Moscow, which were central locations in terms of communications, transportation, and weaponry. These areas, according to Mawdsley, "contained most of the war industry, most establishments and stores of the old army and navy."[1] The Bolsheviks were also successful in raising a sizeable army led by experienced officers, and attracted recruits from the peasant class. Military strength was important, but so was winning support among the people. While the Bolshevik plan for improving Russia was weak, Mawdsley explains, the opposition did not offer a more acceptable platform. Furthermore, there was the significant factor of what is now called the Red Terror, a series of Bolshevik attacks on their political enemies. Mawdsley writes that the Red Terror prevented "internal" revolt within the party and kept the base of Bolshevik power steady.

The Communist leadership in Russia quickly forgot its pledge to establish a coalition socialist government. Instead, Lenin was focused on accumulating power. In 1919, he wrote, "The proletariat must first overthrow the bourgeoisie and win *for itself* state power, that is, the dictatorship of the proletariat, as an instrument of its class for the purpose of winning the sympathy of the majority of the working people."[2] In other words, Lenin cared little for winning popular support. The will of the people mattered less than having power.

Indeed, Lenin had become more and more radical, as many of his contemporaries were beginning to notice. Nikolai Sukhanov, who experienced the revolution as well as its aftermath, defined "genius" in the following way:

> A genius is, as is well known, an "abnormal" person who is "not quite right in the head." More correctly, he is a person with an extremely narrow sphere of mental activity, but who in that sphere works with extraordinary force and productivity. A genius is an extremely narrow person, a chauvinist to the core, who is not receptive to and is unable to understand the most simple and straightforward things.[3]

Nonetheless, the Bolsheviks solidified their power by defeating the opposition and eventually won popular support. Yet, as Sukhanov noted in his portrait of the Communist leader, the majority of Russians were easily won over by coercion because of their virtually nonexistent experience with democracy: "The Bolshevik party was Lenin's work and his alone." He said that Lenin's "shameless radicalism" eventually "guaranteed him success among the proletarian-peasant masses, having no experience other than the tsarist whip."[4]

After winning the civil war, the Communist leadership set about laying down the structure of the new Soviet government. The official ruling party was the Communist Party of the Soviet Union (CPSU). Because most of the country, especially in Moscow and St. Petersburg, already had a system of soviets in place, a Supreme Soviet was established, which would serve as the legislative branch of the new national government and be composed of about 1,500 members. Eventually, the real power would be concentrated in the hands of the Central Committee, a leading body within the CPSU, and its Politburo (or Political Bureau), which was the most powerful force within the party. Although composed of just 13 members, the Politburo had a direct influence on the CPSU's general secretary, the nation's leader.

One of the most troubling aspects of the Bolshevik Revolution was its hypocritical stance on the rights of the proletariat. Lenin had advocated using force to coerce people into following the new system of government. Philosopher Bertrand Russell visited Russia during its civil war and noted the impact of the new regime on intellectual thought. In his book *The Practice and Theory of Bolshevism*, he rejects the Bolshevik way in Russia for many reasons, including its use of force and intimidation to crush rebellion:

> The necessity of inculcating Communism produces a hot-house condition, where every breath of fresh air must be

excluded: people are to be taught to think in a certain way, and all free intelligence becomes taboo.... Every kind of liberty is banned as being *"bourgeois"* but it remains a fact that intelligence languishes where thought is not free.[5]

This stamping out of free thought and individual rights was, as Russell saw it, essential to Bolshevism: "The Bolshevik theory is that a small minority are to seize power, and are to hold it until Communism is accepted practically universally, which, they admit, may take a long time."[6] Here was the essence of Leninism/Bolshevism: the willingness to crush the rights of the proletariat while, at the same time, insisting on the rights of that same group.

JOSEPH STALIN

There is no more controversial figure in the history of the Soviet Union than Joseph Stalin—an ardent believer in Lenin's ideas and in the concept of a strong, authoritarian central government—who ruled from 1922 to 1953. The "Stalinist Terror"—a series of purges, arrests, and killings—is considered by historians to have begun in December 1934, when he had a member of the Politburo, Sergei Kirov, executed (even though Stalin had been eliminating people from the central political party as early as 1929). Kirov's crime was to pose a challenge to Stalin's authority by advocating a relaxation of the leader's harsh policies. According to author Andrei Sinyavsky, the execution of Kirov "marked the beginning of the purges."[7]

Stalin was paranoid about maintaining his grip on power, and he released thousands of spies into the general community to report on people's activities and expressions. The NKVD (which stands in Russian for People's Commissariat for Internal Affairs) became a terror-inspiring, secret police force, carrying out Stalin's orders and investigating people thought to oppose his regime or his policies.

Premier Joseph Stalin is photographed in 1943. Stalin, who ruled the Soviet Union from 1922 to 1953, is one of the most powerful and murderous dictators in world history.

Although he clamped down on opposition, one group, calling itself the Union of Marxists-Leninists, criticized Stalin openly: "A regime of unheard terror and colossal spying, achieved through an extraordinarily centralised and ramified gigantic apparatus, concentrating in its hands all the material resources of the country and placing in direct dependence on itself the physical survival of tens of millions of people, this is the main basis of Stalin's dictatorship."[8] The leader of this group, Mikhail Ryutin, escaped the death penalty, as demanded by Stalin, and was instead sentenced to 10 years in prison.

Sinyavsky explains that like Lenin, Stalin felt it was a great crime, punishable by death, for a person to express loyalty to the bourgeoisie, and "even the mildest criticism of the State and Stalin was regarded as bourgeois agitation and propaganda." Furthermore, he adds, "This criticism didn't have to be uttered: the suspicion of an unorthodox thought was enough; a slip of the tongue or a misprint was ample."[9] Millions were arrested and killed in the Stalinist terror, and a great oppression settled upon the Russian people, who were afraid to utter their thoughts freely lest their lives and families be placed in danger.

This result hardly seemed to meet the goals of the great revolution, which had argued that the working class should determine its own future. Stalin had betrayed the aims of the revolution; in fact, many of the people he executed or had arrested were former political leaders of the revolution. In addition to attacking critics within the government, Stalin's regime also cracked down more harshly than ever on the Russian Orthodox Church, to ensure that the Church did not gain or solidify any power. All power in Russia had to be centralized under the bureaucracy and—therefore under Stalin himself.

Many intellectuals criticized Stalin's terror and centralization of power only mildly, including Leon Trotsky himself. In *The Revolution Betrayed*, Trotsky explained that Russia had made great progress as a nation under Communism and had finally put power into the hands of the proletariat, but this achievement had been somewhat weakened by Stalin. He felt, however, that the bureaucracy had to take a strong role because Russia, due to poverty and illiteracy, was still behind other nations; he argued, "The present Soviet society cannot get along without a state, nor even—within limits— without a bureaucracy."[10] Therefore, while Stalin's regime was troubling and did not mark the achievement of the revolution's dream of a Communist state, Trotsky believed it was still in transition to that ideal, future state. Stalin's problematic regime would be eclipsed by a future revival of the revolution, he believed, which would occur on a wider scale, in Europe and beyond.

Others were more harsh in their assessment of Stalin: In a letter to Stalin himself, one former party member, Fedor Raskolnikov, wrote: "You have destroyed the party of Lenin, and on its bones you have built a new 'party of Lenin and Stalin,' which serves as a cover for your one-man rule. . . . The list of your crimes is endless. The list of your victims is endless."[11] Written in 1939 after his escape from Russia, Raskolnikov's letter also claimed that Stalin's version of socialism was a far cry from "true socialism," or the socialist ideal that had been the basis of the 1917 revolution.

THE SOVIET ECONOMY

The Soviet economy slowly strengthened, despite the fact that morale waned under Stalin. Since 1929, the government had imposed a system known as the "command economy." The Soviet economy was carefully organized and planned by government agencies; these agencies tried to control the market and market prices by setting quotas for production by Soviet industries and agricultural sectors. This was meant to employ more people, increase production rates in the USSR, and, of course, demonstrate to the capitalist West that a carefully controlled economy was preferable to a free market system.

Stalin also imposed another system, known as collectivization, in which the government established labor camps for agricultural work. Peasants and members of the lowest classes were forced to work in these camps, their collective labor contributing to the meeting of the production quotas, but millions died from inhumane and violent treatment in the process. It was yet another brutal policy that would become part of Stalin's legacy.

JOSEPH STALIN

Joseph Stalin was born Iosif Vissarionovich Dzhugashvili in 1879 in a small town in Georgia, a former Soviet republic that is now a separate nation. His father was a cobbler and his mother cleaned houses; his other two older siblings died, leaving Joseph an only child. Showing academic promise, he was awarded a scholarship to a local Orthodox seminary in 1894.

Despite his deep faith, five years later he had renounced religion and joined the revolution against the monarchy, having been convinced by his readings of Karl Marx that socialism was the way forward and the best hope for the nation. His new political affiliation landed him in trouble with the religious authorities, especially as he worked with local socialist organizations to spread the ideas of the new movement. In 1903, Stalin was attracted to Lenin's Bolshevik socialist movement and he became even more active, causing him to be arrested and exiled several times. After Lenin appointed him to high posts within the Bolshevik Party, Stalin wrote a noted theoretical essay, "Marxism and the National Question." In 1917, following the Bolshevik Revolution, Stalin was appointed to the Central Committee and later to the Politburo. During the Russian Civil War, he proved himself to be a skilled military strategist. After the Bolsheviks had won and the Soviet Union was established, he achieved the

THE PATRIOTIC WAR

As Stalin was organizing the Soviet state to suit his vision, Russia's old rival Germany was beginning to assert itself again after its defeat in World War I. The startling rise of Adolf

highest rank when he was named general secretary of the Communist Party.

Despite his rapid rise, Stalin's behavior caused others around him to be concerned and even alarmed. He had already made an enemy of Leon Trotsky and, as Amy Knight writes, "Stalin's rude and aggressive behavior brought him into conflict with the ailing Lenin, who shortly before his death in 1924 wrote his political 'testament' in which he voiced misgivings about Stalin. In the testament Lenin expressed doubt whether the party's general secretary would use his authority with sufficient caution, and he called for Stalin's removal from the post."[*] While Stalin successfully suppressed Lenin's criticism of his governing style, it is interesting to note that his colleagues had registered such strong misgivings about him.

During his time in power, Stalin showed little regard for the welfare of the people he governed. The industrialization program he promoted caused much suffering and misery; peasants who had been organized into collective farms were not provided for in terms of food and care, and many died. His squads of secret police wreaked havoc on average citizens, who lived in fear of being accused of disloyalty to Stalin's regime and programs. His terror, says Knight, "left a permanent scar on the collective memory of the people under his rule."[**]

---

[*] Amy Knight, MSN Encarta Encyclopedia, 2008. http://www.encarta.msn.com/text_761559200_0/stalin.html.

[**] Ibid.

Hitler's fascist Nazi Party had made Stalin and other world leaders concerned, but Stalin felt he had no real reason to fear Hitler or to fear an attack by Germany. After all, in 1939, the two nations had signed a nonaggression treaty, and Stalin and the Russians watched passively as Hitler and the German army conquered much of Europe, including France.

On June 22, 1941, however, the Soviet Union was surprised by the invasion of its land by the German army. The finest of the Soviet Union's military forces, which had been stationed along the German border, were destroyed in the first few days of the Nazi attack. Its air force was also nearly eradicated; most planes never even had a chance to leave the ground. The Nazis succeeded in seizing sizeable tracts of Soviet territory and continued to push forward aggressively. When news of the attack reached Stalin, he immediately realized that he needed the support and total loyalty of the population to avoid succumbing to Hitler's forces. Stalin knew that Hitler would have an easier time defeating the USSR if its citizens were eager to overthrow their leader. Therefore, Stalin had to rally the population, which had hated him and had detested his brutal policies for more than a decade. Convincing them that he was their champion would not be an easy task.

The shift in tone—from focusing on the power of the bureaucracy to emphasizing the unity of the people—can be seen in the radio broadcast announcing the German attack:

> This is not the first time that our people [have] had to deal with an attacking enemy. Our people responded to Napoleon's campaign in Russian with the Patriotic War, and Napoleon was defeated and ultimately destroyed. And the same will happen to the arrogant Hitler, declaring a new campaign against our country. The Red Army and our whole people will once again conduct a victorious Patriotic War for the Motherland, for honour, for freedom.... The government calls on you, citizens of the Soviet Union, to unite even closer

Two German soldiers are seen on the front lines in 1941, during the early days of the German invasion of the Soviet Union.

around our glorious Bolshevik party, around our Soviet government, around our great leader Comrade Stalin.[12]

In his first radio address to the people, more than a week after the attack, Stalin himself emphasized the need for unity and linked the struggle against Germany with the same struggle of the Western powers:

> The war with fascist Germany cannot be considered an ordinary war. It is not only a war between two armies, it is also a great war of the entire Soviet people against the German-fascist armies. . . . Our war for the freedom of our country will merge with the struggle of the peoples of Europe and America for their independence, for democratic liberties.

It will be a united front of the peoples standing for freedom against enslavement and threats of enslavement by Hitler's fascist armies.[13]

Richard Sakwa explains that this focus on the common struggle, with the Western powers, for "democratic liberties" was a hint by Stalin to his people that reform would be in the USSR's future if Germany were defeated. It also seems to be a reminder to the people that life under German fascism would be much worse than it had been under Stalin's regime, that the German plan was to exterminate the Russian ethnic population and replace it with the Aryan race, the "ideal" race, according to Nazi beliefs.

In the days and weeks that followed, the aura of Stalinist-style Communism was strategically replaced by one of patriotism: as Sakwa points out, for example, the Communist slogan, "Proletarians of the world, unite," featured prominently on most Soviet newspapers, was replaced by "Death to the German occupier."[14] Everywhere, the focus shifted from Communist ideology to patriotism and loyalty to the motherland. Stalin even relaxed his policies on the Russian Orthodox Church, hoping to use it as a way to garner additional support. A proclamation by the Church leaders stated: "Let the Heavenly Head of the Church bless the works of the Government with the Creator's blessing and let him crown our struggle in a just cause with the victory we long for and the liberation of suffering humanity from the dark bondage of fascism."[15]

Indeed, as Sakwa explains, there were two wars going on: one pitting the USSR against Germany and an internal effort by Stalin to maintain his hold on power. He needed the people to rally around him, rather than greet the Germans as liberators. The brutality of the German army toward the Russian people, especially to Jews, in territories it occupied, helped sway the people's favor toward Stalin and increased resistance toward the Nazis. It is estimated that 20 million citizens of the Soviet

Union, Russians as well as other ethnic groups, died fighting the Nazis in World War II.

The tide of the war eventually turned in favor of the Soviet Union. The German attempt to take over Moscow in November 1941 was rebuffed, and the Nazis suddenly found themselves facing the harsh Russian winter, for which they were woefully unprepared. The cold winds and icy temperatures caused German vehicles and tanks to freeze in the mud, dealing a blow not only to the Nazi effort to advance but leading to their eventual defeat. It was not until April 1944 that the last remnants of the German army were ousted from Soviet soil and the USSR was liberated. Hitler died by his own hand in April 1945 and his Third Reich surrendered in May. World War II came to an end in August 1945, after the surrender of Germany's ally, Japan.

5

The Cold War
with the West

D espite the hopes of the common people, Stalin hardly
lived up to his wartime promises to secure democracy
or relax his brutal policies. Even before the war had ended, he
saw to the expulsion of hundreds of thousands of peoples of
various ethnic groups, including the Tatars, the Chechens, the
Ingush, and others, from their homes in the Crimean region
and in the Caucuses, under suspicion that they had betrayed
the USSR's defensive efforts and aided the Germans. They were
rounded up and transported to Central Asia, where many of
them did not survive the rough conditions.

By the end of the war, the USSR had regained all of its terri-
tory seized by the Germans, as well as additional land in Eastern
Europe, including all or parts of Romania, Bulgaria, Hungary,
East Germany (including the eastern part of Berlin, the German

capital), Poland, and Czechoslovakia. In other words, the Patriotic War, as Stalin had described World War II to his people, had brought not only the elimination of German aggression, but the acquisition of new territory to add to the Soviet Empire.

To the chagrin of the Western powers, namely the United States and Great Britain, it became obvious that Stalin did not want to cede any of the land the USSR had occupied during the war. In fact, it was clear that rather than restore the governments of those countries, he wanted to make them Communist puppet states and thus expand the Soviet influence into Eastern Europe. The fact that the USSR already occupied those lands made it difficult for the Western powers to force Stalin to remove his troops. According to Thomas Wolfe, Stalin was surely aware that the presence of his military would help to influence how boundary lines would be drawn in Europe.[1]

In postwar negotiations among the Allies, the USSR was able to carve out a "sphere of influence" (an area or region where another state or organization has power) in Eastern Europe. From the beginning, the United States, as a democratic society, wanted the occupied Eastern European nations to be self-governed. In a speech delivered on March 12, 1947, President Harry Truman adopted the policy of containment by declaring that the United States would not tolerate the expansion of Communism into Eastern Europe.

The Cold War between the West and the Soviet Union would begin that summer, when Stalin thwarted Western attempts to establish the Europe Recovery Program, informally known as the Marshall Plan, after the plan's primary architect, U.S. Secretary of State George C. Marshall. The meeting of the involved nations was scheduled to be held in Paris in June 1947, but Stalin decided that the Soviet Union would not participate; furthermore, he forbade representatives from Poland and Czechoslovakia to attend as well. The Western powers were angered by the move, which made it clear that Stalin had no interest in establishing peaceful, cooperative relations. Perhaps, as Richard Sakwa points out, Stalin realized that he needed an enemy against which the Soviets could rally, so as to distract from his own unpopular policies and unite the nation behind him.[2] As it had been before World War II, the enemy would once again be the capitalist West.

THE COLD WAR ERA

Many historians agree that Joseph Stalin helped to trigger the Cold War, the era of hostility and tension between the Communist East (led by the Soviet Union) and the democratic capitalist West (led by the United States). This rivalry would dominate international politics for five decades. The brief era of cooperation between East and West had ended with the defeat of the Axis Powers of Germany, Japan, and Italy.

On March 5, 1946, former British Prime Minister Winston Churchill gave his famous "Sinews of Peace" speech, which is popularly known as the "Iron Curtain" speech. Speaking at Westminster College, in Missouri, he said in part:

> From Stettin in the Baltic to Trieste in the Adriatic, an iron curtain has descended across the Continent. Behind that line lie all the capitals of the ancient states of Central and Eastern Europe. Warsaw, Berlin, Prague, Vienna, Budapest, Belgrade, Bucharest and Sofia, all these famous cities and the populations around them lie in what I must call the Soviet sphere, and all are subject in one form or another, not only to Soviet influence but to a very high and, in many cases, increasing measure of control from Moscow.[3]

The speech brought the term "iron curtain" into popular usage as a way to describe the cultural, economic, and ideological separation between capitalist and Communist European nations. After the Soviet Union withdrew from the Paris conference, Stalin set out to build a Communist Russian empire. Philip Longworth describes the "construction of a new kind of Russian empire consisting of nominally independent dominions"[4]—in other words, the new territory acquired during World War II would be the new client states of the empire. These countries included Albania, Poland, Czechoslovakia, Hungary, Bulgaria, East Germany, and Romania.

The Warsaw Pact, signed in 1955, created a "treaty of friendship, co-operation and mutual assistance" between the Soviet Union and these nations. Part of the agreement included establishing a joint command for their armed forces, which in effect allowed the Soviet Union to dominate these countries militarily. These client states, collectively referred to as the Eastern Bloc states, were therefore forcibly joined to the USSR. Longworth explains that their governments "were transformed into obedient satellites following policies of planned production, collectivization of farming, and obedience to Moscow's political line."[5]

These Eastern European states, unwilling members of the new Communist Empire, were often resistant to the imposition of a new ideology on their citizens. According to Longworth, they were controlled by the Soviets via three "channels" or methods: first, through what he calls "diplomatic relations"; second, through compliance with the policies of the USSR's Communist Party by all political parties within these states; and third, through a system of "security services," which means the secret police, that used a vast network of spies and agents to instill fear in the general population and suppress dissent.[6]

During the Cold War, the USSR, beginning with Stalin, emphasized the building and stockpiling of nuclear weapons as a way to defend itself against future attack by the Western powers. Additionally, because World War II had drained the Soviet economy of material and manpower, the USSR exploited the economies of its new client states to bolster its own dwindling reserves. Work and production quotas were set on the workers and facilities of these states. After 1950, the economic relationship between the USSR and these states became more stable and, according to William E. Watson, "they were guaranteed certain economic and military subsidies from the USSR—such as guaranteed purchases of their products at artificially high process, and cheap weapons systems."[7]

NIKITA KHRUSHCHEV

In 1953, Joseph Stalin died and was succeeded by another soon-to-be legendary leader, Nikita Khrushchev, who seemed to present a turning point in Soviet politics. In 1956, he began to implement de-Stalinization policies. He publicly criticized Joseph Stalin's reign of terror, especially because of its devastating impact on the morale of members of the Communist Party. Meant to rectify some of the damage done to the party by Stalin, "destalinization signaled a lessening of the hard-line party control over the artistic, educational, and scientific establishments within the Soviet Union, and the end of the terrorizing of the party by the political police," Watson writes.[8] Little else, however, changed inside or outside the Soviet Union: The USSR continued its economic and military competition with the United States, set production quotas of workers in satellite states, and used its secret police systems against the citizens of its empire.

The Hungarian Revolution of 1956 displayed the first cracks in the iron curtain to the West. Between October 23 and November 10, 1956, Hungarians revolted against the Stalinist policies of the Soviet government. What began as a student demonstration in Budapest, the Hungarian capital, quickly erupted into national revolution. Militias of private citizens battled with the state police and Soviet forces, and attempted to topple the Communist government and install a new government in its place, one that declared independence from the USSR. On November 4, the Politburo charged the Soviet army with suppressing the revolution; the invasion of Hungary began immediately. All told, an estimated 2,500 Hungarians had been

Soviet Premier Nikita Khrushchev pounds his fist while addressing the United Nations General Assembly in New York City on October 3, 1960.

killed and many more imprisoned in this revolution; tens of thousands more became refugees. By January 1957, all remaining protests and pocket groups of revolutionaries had been ferreted out and crushed as well. The Soviets then reinstalled the Communist government.

In October 1962, the USSR, under Khrushchev, faced 13 harrowing days as it came close to having a nuclear confrontation with the United States. On October 14, U.S. spy planes discovered that the Soviet Union had set up nuclear launch sites on the island of Cuba, a Communist country 90 miles (144.8 km) from the U.S. mainland. U.S. President John F. Kennedy ordered an immediate blockade of the island to prevent Soviet ships from adding to the nuclear arsenal already in Cuba. Kennedy's move forced Khrushchev to make a decision: Would he order Soviet ships to run the American blockade and possibly trigger a nuclear war, or would the ships turn back?

Kennedy and Khrushchev had already had a difficult face-to-face meeting in Vienna, Austria, in 1961, and both men left that summit with a sour impression of the other. Khrushchev had found the young American president to be rather soft on many issues and came away with the idea that he could take advantage of Kennedy. During the Cuban Missile Crisis, however, Kennedy presented his tougher side to the Soviet leader. On October 24, the Soviet ships stopped short of the blockade line. After two intense days of negotiations, the crisis ended and nuclear war was averted: The Soviet Union agreed to remove its missile sites from Cuba in exchange for U.S. promises not to invade Cuba and to pull its own nuclear missiles out of Turkey, close to the Soviet border. Khrushchev's removal of Soviet missiles from Cuba cost him much prestige among Russians. In 1964, he was ousted by members of the Communist Party. As Watson says, "Party leaders still equated the internal success of the Soviet Union with Cold War successes abroad."[9]

THE PRAGUE SPRING

Although life for people in the USSR continued to be difficult, Philip Longworth notes, "By the 1970s the population of the Soviet Union was better fed, better housed and enjoyed a higher real standard of living than it had ever done."[10] With the economy in relatively good shape, Khrushchev's successor, Leonid Brezhnev, focused on strengthening the USSR militarily. Much money was spent on defense measures, building a nuclear arsenal and other weaponry, which helped to increase employment. These weapons would be needed in the summer of 1968, when the Soviet military was sent into action after a revolt broke out in Czechoslovakia, one of the Warsaw Pact states.

In January of that year, a new Czech leader came to power, Alexander Dubček of the Communist Party of Czechoslovakia. He wanted to enact reforms, known as the Prague Spring reforms, that would allow Czech citizens free speech and access to a less-censored media, among other liberalizing measures. Dubček's ideas alarmed leaders in Moscow, who warned that talk of democratic reform was an attack on the socialist ideology of the USSR. Brezhnev and the Politburo were not reassured by Dubček's insistence that the Warsaw Pact and Communist ideology in the client states were not in danger.

When negotiations with Dubček and Moscow failed, Brezhnev ordered a Soviet invasion of Czechoslovakia in late August 1968. More than 200,000 troops quickly conquered and occupied Czechoslovakia. Hundreds of thousands of Czechs fled, causing an emigration problem, and many others protested the occupation. Dubček was arrested but eventually permitted to remain in office and continue with less radical reforms. The revolt and the Soviet military response gave rise to the Brezhnev Doctrine, which David R. Marples describes as a policy "whereby the Soviet Union (and Soviet bloc countries) would not permit a Communist state to be overthrown from within, on the grounds that the government in question had been chosen by the 'people.'"[11] In other words, it established the right of the USSR to militarily intervene when a client state's government was not complying with the policies of the CPSU.

ECONOMIC PARALYSIS

Despite all his military spending, Brezhnev failed to focus on long-term economic growth and, as Longworth states, "the Soviet economy had been unable to compete with capitalism"[12] since the 1960s. Jeremy Smith notes, "By 1973-74, the Soviet economy had entered a marked slowdown, and by the 1980s the economy had almost ceased to grow altogether."[13]

A demonstrator in Prague holds the Czech national flag in front of a Soviet tank on August 23, 1968. Although the Prague Spring was brutally suppressed by invading Soviet forces, the reform effort showed the rest of the world the growing rifts inside the Soviet sphere of influence.

One of the major problems facing Brezhnev was the size of the Soviet government, which encompassed an enormous bureaucracy that Longworth calls the "apparatchiki," or the "Soviet managerial class."[14] William Watson describes this group in more detail, explaining that the government was swollen by "tens of thousands of high-ranking party officials" who, in exchange for their loyalty to the party, were kept happy with certain privileges. Under Brezhnev, their numbers had increased and so had their perks, including luxury residences, educational opportunities, and other benefits.

Because the Soviet economy had done well in the 1950s and 1960s, a new professional, educated class of Soviet citizens had emerged, which included doctors and lawyers. This group had grown dissatisfied with the Communist system under which they lived. Jeremy Smith writes,

> Members of this social group were denied the relatively higher earnings of their equivalents in the West, and were also more disturbed by the absence of political rights and freedom of speech . . . it was above all the professionals who formed the social basis for reform and who had the most to gain from radical change.[15]

David R. Marples similarly highlights the growth of a group of dissidents from the 1960s onward who "notes the gap between the theoretical basis of Soviet power and the way that it was exercised."[16] For these Soviets and others, it was easy to predict a future crisis: The USSR had a strong military but a weak economy, a tight grip on individual rights, a swollen government that was becoming corrupt and ineffective, and increasing agitation within many of its satellite states.

In the late 1960s, the USSR unofficially entered into the Vietnam War, the civil war between Communist North Vietnam and capitalist South Vietnam. Because the Soviet Union wanted to influence the Asian region, it armed the North, whose army was known as the Viet Cong. This prompted the United States to come to the aid of the South Vietnamese as a way to balance the Communist influence. The superpowers used Vietnam as a proxy war to wage their ideological battles. Confronted with protests over the war at home and a tenacious enemy in the Viet Cong, the Unites States withdrew its forces in 1973. South Vietnam was defeated by North Vietnam two years later. The war had an effect on all of Southeast Asia, in which Leonid Brezhnev hoped to carve out a further sphere of influence and expand the Communist Empire. Communist Vietnam soon defeated Laos and Cambodia, bringing those neighboring nations under Communist control as well.

COLD WAR DIPLOMACY

Diplomacy between the Soviet Union and the United States during the Cold War was an interesting puzzle. The rivalry generated intense competition in almost every arena: politics, the nuclear arms race, space exploration, even the arts and education. When members of either side confronted the other in a diplomatic setting, the tension was palpable.

Some of the most colorful diplomatic confrontations occurred at the United Nations, where the United States and the USSR each held a permanent seat on the Security Council. In 1960, Soviet Premier Nikita Khrushchev took off one of his shoes and banged it on the table in frustration. During the Cuban Missile Crisis of 1962, U.S. Ambassador to the United Nations Adlai Stevenson confronted the Soviet representative, Valerian Zorin, with photographs that proved the existence of missiles in Cuba just moments after Zorin had suggested they did not exist.

The USSR under Brezhnev also tried to have an influence in the Middle East. The Egyptians, led by the charismatic Gamal Abdel Nasser, had ousted their Western-friendly monarch, King Farouk, in 1952. Nasser tried to establish a relationship with the United States, but when rebuffed, he turned toward the Soviet Union. The Soviets were happy to arm Nasser as a way of building influence in the region, which prompted the United States to form an alliance with Israel as a way to balance Soviet influence.

Despite these efforts to grow Communism in Asia and the Middle East, the USSR could not continue to expand militarily while declining economically. For example, it paid billions of

Much of the Cold War, however, was simply a battle of ideas. The United States often used media outlets to transmit the ideals of democracy, freedom, and human rights. Radio stations such as Voice of America (VOA) and United States Information Agency (USIA) fed ideas about the benefits of living in a free society to Communist-led countries in an effort to stir uprisings against the Soviet grip on power. During his administration, President Jimmy Carter emphasized the issue of human rights around the world as a way of spreading these ideals to the Soviet Union. His national security advisor, Zbigniew Brzezinski, often pitted the American ideal of human rights against Soviet military aggression, especially following the Soviet invasion of Afghanistan. Carter's successor, Ronald Reagan, took this theme even further: His famous speech at the Brandenburg Gate, in which he called upon the Soviet government to tear down the Berlin Wall, helped strengthen the idea that America and the West cherished liberty, in contrast to the fear, censorship, and authoritarianism practiced by the Soviet Union.

rubles a year to Soviet-friendly states; Vietnam alone received one billion rubles a year for granting Soviet ships access to its ports in the Pacific and Indian oceans.[17] Although the USSR's conventional forces and nuclear stockpiles were often comparable to those in the United States, its economy was very weak compared with that of its greatest rival. As Jeremy Smith notes, the emphasis on stockpiling arms "severely restricted the room for improvement in other areas of the economy."[18]

A COSTLY WAR
In December 1979, Brezhnev decided to invade the neighboring country of Afghanistan. In an effort to continue spreading Communist ideals, the USSR invaded Afghanistan in 1978 and established the Democratic Republic of Afghanistan. This new government provoked much revolt within the country, especially from the mujahedin—Islamic military fighters who sought to liberate the country from a Communist power in the name of Islam. (Among other reasons, the mujahedin objected to a Communist government because it was necessarily an atheist one, which did not suit a religious, Islamic population.) The new republic continued to receive aid from the USSR, but the mujahedin began to overwhelm its resources.

Why was Afghanistan so important to the USSR? William Watson says, "The Soviets clearly hoped to gain Afghanistan as a client state. Their interest in the country was partly based on Afghanistan's location along their own border, and partly because it would put them within striking distance of the Persian Gulf and India."[19] Brezhnev decided that the Soviet military needed to defeat the mujahedin rebels and secure Afghanistan as a client state. Richard Sakwa notes that many academics and officials in the government warned Brezhnev that the invasion was a bad idea, but he proceeded with it nevertheless. Brezhnev miscalculated the Afghan response to the invasion, however, and it would prove a costly mistake.

Given the massive buildup of the military and weapons by the USSR under Brezhnev, there was little reason to imagine that the Afghans, a population of poorly educated people of various ethnic tribes, most of whom lived in poverty, could put up much of a fight. Just as the Germans had not been able to tackle the Russian winter during World War II, however, the Soviets were stymied by the rough Afghan mountain terrain by the early 1980s. Before long, the Soviets were mired in a conflict that was impossible to win; the death toll mounted and the finances began to mount as the Soviet military tried to hold its tenuous occupation of a country fraught with rebels. The war with Afghanistan earned the USSR severe criticism at home and abroad.

The Era of
Gorbachev

B rezhnev, who had presided over an era of military expansion, economic stagnation, and massive internal corruption, died in 1982. He was succeeded by Yuri Andropov, the head of the KGB—the Soviets' elite secret police, internal security, and espionage organization. Andropov intended to end Brezhnev's rampant corruption by putting restrictions on the apparatchikis, but he became ill. During his illness, he was aided in many of his duties by a young member of the Politburo, Mikhail Gorbachev. Andropov died suddenly in early 1984.

Despite the backing by many members of the Politburo of Gorbachev for the position of general secretary, Andropov's successor was Konstantin Chernenko, who was a follower of Brezhnev's policies; Chernenko effectively set back many of Andropov's attempts to reform the government, as many had feared. As William Watson affirms, "During Chernenko's 13-month tenure as general secretary, the Brezhnev status quo was temporarily restored."[1] He focused on military issues, such as the occupation of Afghanistan, rather than on the withering economy, and took a hard line with dealing with the client states. Because Chernenko was in his early seventies and not in the best of health when he was named head of the party, it was hardly a surprise to anyone when he died in office in 1985. With Chernenko's death, the Politburo turned to Gorbachev. In 1980, at the age of 49, he had been named to membership in the Politburo. By the mid-1980s, he was seen as a rising young star within the party and had forged alliances and good faith with many of the younger officials. He was primarily known as a positive force in the agricultural sector, but he also displayed keen awareness of party politics and governance.

Gorbachev was named general secretary of the CPSU on March 10, 1985. Philip Longworth notes, "Gorbachev was a new kind of Soviet leader. As outgoing as Khrushchev, though less crude and excitable, he was ready to engage with the public and made a point of encouraging debate."[2] Indeed, Gorbachev had long been of the mind that the USSR needed major reform from within to keep it competitive with other nations and to improve the status quo among its citizens. The problem was how to implement this kind of change: How much change could the empire tolerate in the face of all its challenges? These challenges included an ongoing war with Afghanistan, rebellions in the satellite states, a large and expensive military, a weakening economy (because of the costs of maintaining an empire as well as sharply rising oil prices in the 1970s), a long history of political suppression, and a poor impression of Soviet tactics and politics in other countries.

Gorbachev was able to work on the last issue almost immediately. British Prime Minister Margaret Thatcher met him in December 1984 during Gorbachev's visit to her country. She later said of him, "I like Mr. Gorbachev. We can do business together."[3] Other world leaders had similar impressions of the young Soviet leader; they generally found him to be open-minded and flexible, but keenly intelligent and perceptive. He was not one of the "old guard" like Brezhnev and Chernenko; he was more modern in his approach to government and diplomacy. In fact, early in the winter of 1986, at the Twenty-seventh Congress of the CPSU, Gorbachev publicly criticized the political reign of Leonid Brezhnev, calling it the "Epoch of Stagnation," which signaled that he would move in a different, more positive direction. This move was welcomed by leaders in other countries.

In December 1986, Gorbachev ordered the release of Andrei Sakharov, a Soviet dissident who had been calling for greater human and civil rights in the USSR since the 1960s. Sakharov, who was a physicist by training, had been held under house arrest since 1980, but the media-savvy man was known internationally for his cause. His wife, Yelena Bonner, a poet and also an activist, had been in prison for some time as well; Gorbachev released her, too. While Sakharov's release made waves in the USSR, it also had a major effect abroad. Jeremy Smith notes, "His release immediately raised Gorbachev's stock in the estimation of politicians and commentators in the West, who now for the first time began to suspect that something truly different was happening in the USSR."[4]

Gorbachev also began reforming the CPSU from inside the party. Smith notes that within Gorbachev's first months as general secretary, he removed many of the older members of the CPSU from their posts, especially those officials who had been staunch supporters of Brezhnev. Some of the new, younger officials he appointed included Eduard Shevardnadze, who was appointed the foreign minister, and Boris Yeltsin, who became head of the Communist Party in Moscow. "By 1988," Smith writes, "66 percent of the members of the Party's Central Committee had been appointed in

British Prime Minister Margaret Thatcher and Mikhail Gorbachev in 1987. Following their first meeting in 1984, Thatcher declared that she could "do business" with the new Soviet president.

Gorbachev's time, and most remaining members of the 'old guard' were forced out in the following year."[5] Radical change had begun, it seemed.

U.S. President Ronald Reagan was also keenly interested in Mikhail Gorbachev, but would initially have a tense and difficult working relationship with him. Reagan, a conservative cold warrior and member of the Republican Party, was wildly popular among Americans for his charisma and wit, as well as his seeming directness in dealing with other leaders and dignitaries. Reagan believed the best way to deal with the Soviet Union was by direct challenge, which included the stockpiling of nuclear arms, because he believed the Soviet economy could not compete with America's supply.

(continues on page 68)

MIKHAIL GORBACHEV

Despite his best efforts to reform the Soviet Union, Mikhail Sergeyevich Gorbachev helped to bring about the downfall of the Soviet empire.

Gorbachev, or "Gorby" as he was known in the American press, was born on March 2, 1931, in the village of Privolnoe in southern Russia. His father worked in agriculture, driving a tractor on one of Stalin's collective farms. His family had suffered during the Stalin regime: One grandfather incurred Stalin's wrath in 1933 by failing to meet a crop-sowing plan and was imprisoned and then exiled; in 1937, his other grandfather was accused of political actions against Stalin's regime and executed.* Gorbachev's father had been sent to fight in World War II, and, as Jeremy Smith explains, "the young Mikhail was burdened with family responsibilities at the early age of 11."** Because the German army occupied Privolnoe during the war, Gorbachev witnessed some of the horror inflicted upon the population by the Nazis.

At the age of 15, Gorbachev went to work in the agricultural sector. Like many teenagers, he joined the Communist Youth League, known as the Komsomol. When he was 18, he was recognized by the youth league for his hard work and awarded the Red Banner of Labor.*** He officially joined the Communist Party shortly after enrolling as a law student at Moscow State University, from which he graduated in 1955. His law degree helped him to understand the contrast between socialist ideals and their actual implementation. Returning to his hometown, he became involved in the administration of the Komsomol, eventually becoming its highest official from the Stavropol region. In 1966, he became secretary of the Stavropol City

Committee of the CPSU. He graduated with a degree in economics from the Stavropol Agricultural Institute in 1967, and continued to climb through the ranks of the party. In 1970, he rose to the prestigious position of first secretary of the Stavropol region's Committee of the CPSU. He was responsible for governing the region, which had a population of 2.4 million.[†]

William E. Watson explains that it was in that same year, 1970, that Gorbachev began his "ascent to the highest level of power," by becoming one of the 1,500 elected members of the Supreme Soviet. "In the following year," Watson writes, "at the Twenty-Fourth Party Congress, he was elected a member of the elite 300-member Central Committee." He gleaned much important experience at this time about the inner workings of the Communist Party as the Central Committee was, in Watson's words, the "body [that] governed the daily operation of the party between the party congresses."[‡] It was also a way to make his name known to established party leaders.

As a member of the national party, Gorbachev became known for his ideas on agricultural reforms. Gorbachev saw that the USSR could reduce its dependence on food imports by growing more of its own food. In the late 1970s, he received the Order of the October Revolution, a coveted honor awarded by the CPSU for his work on the Ipatovsky Experiment, a successful agricultural project he had supervised. In 1978, he was named head of the Central Committee's agricultural division; that same year, he was named secretary of the Central Committee.

He became an alternate member of the Politburo in 1979, then a full member, one of 13, in 1980. He was the youngest person to be named a Politburo member

(continues)

(continued)

in Soviet history, and his selection made others hopeful that the Communist Party was ready for fresh ideas. His rise through the party ranks had been swift, but steady, because he had solidified a core group of supporters during his climb.

* Jeremy Smith, *The Fall of Communism: 1985-1991*. New York: Palgrave MacMillan, 2005, p. 23.

** Ibid.

*** William E. Watson, *The Collapse of Communism in the Soviet Union*. Westport, Conn.: Greenwood Press, 1990, p. 65.

† Nobel Prize Biography. http://nobelprize.org/nobel_prizes/peace/laureates/1990/gorbachev-bio.html

‡ Watson, p. 66.

(continued from page 65)

Reagan would prove to be a tough negotiating partner. Gorbachev was tough as well, but he also was in a difficult position. He had learned, as a young man rising through party ranks, that reform on a massive and radical scale was impossible. In fact, Jeremy Smith notes that Gorbachev had been reform-minded from a young age; however, in order to avoid becoming an outsider with the party's leaders and to aid his personal ambitions, he refrained from advocating change too radically or assertively. While the position of general secretary held an immense amount of power, Smith notes, it was not an untouchable position: Nikita Khrushchev had been successfully ousted by the party for what it perceived as his failures. Gorbachev, who wanted to avoid a similar fate, was walking a fine line between those in the party who saw that change was needed and those who felt that change was an impossible or unattractive path.

GORBACHEV'S POLICIES

Before becoming general secretary, Gorbachev had, in public speeches and in articles, mentioned the ideas of perestroika and *uskorenie*. Later, also before becoming the Soviet leader, he added the third of his major policy ideas: glasnost. The combination of these three ideas would form the basis of his efforts to reform the USSR during his tenure as general secretary.

Uskorenie referred to accelerating production as a way of solving the USSR's economic woes. Gorbachev wanted to decrease the country's dependence on imports, and also strengthen the economy by improving production rates. He found that the key to achieving this was by offering workers more independence, an idea probably gleaned from his own family's experiences in the agricultural sector as well as from his years as an administrator in that same sector. While uskorenie was an important part of Gorbachev's platform, his major reform plans were embodied in perestroika and glasnost. Perestroika literally means "restructuring," but is a term widely used in the West to describe Gorbachev's vision of reforming the Soviet economy and society. Jeremy Smith notes that, in Gorbachev's 1987 book *Perestroika: New Thinking for Our Country and the World*, the Soviet leader outlined his ideas for restructuring. Gorbachev noted that during the 1970s, "the country began to lose momentum,"[6] in economic and cultural progress. The rippling effect caused stagnation in other sectors, until "the needs and opinions of ordinary working people, of the public at large, were ignored." Because of this, public morale began to erode, and "the great feeling of solidarity with each other that was forged during the heroic times of the Revolution, the first five-year plans, the Great Patriotic War and postwar rehabilitation was weakening." Author Richard Sakwa also quotes from Gorbachev's book, noting that Gorbachev believed that, "On the whole, society was becoming increasingly unmanageable."[7] Gorbachev argued that change was needed—perestroika was needed—to rejuvenate the system and make the nation's citizens once again involved.

In reforming the political structure of the USSR, the terms "the democratization of society" were employed, to the surprise of many. In fact, as Gorbachev later wrote, it was important to make sure that "every leader, every executive should permanently feel his responsibility to and dependence on the electors, the work collectives, public organizations, the Party and the people as a whole"[8]—in other words, leaders of the CPSU needed to understand that their power was derived from the people whom they represented.

Glasnost meant "openness," indicating Gorbachev's desire to make the Soviet system a more open one, where people could eventually express their ideas freely and openly As David Marples explains, years of political suppression had made it taboo for Soviet citizens to speak about many subjects, including crime, corruption, the economy, and societal problems. The restrictions placed on expression prevented meaningful discussions of these issues from being presented in the media, a source of great angst to the nation's intellectuals, journalists, and writers.

While Gorbachev's training as a lawyer made him concerned about the lack of civil rights and free expression in Soviet society—as well as the experiences of his own family members under Stalin's regime—the events of April 26, 1986 helped to propel his policies on glasnost.

CHERNOBYL

Around 1:30 that morning, an experiment conducted by poorly trained operators led to a massive explosion at a nuclear reactor unit in Chernobyl, a power station located near the city of Kiev, in northern Ukraine. Because a technician had performed a safety experiment after some of the equipment had been turned off, a flaw in the technology allowed the nuclear reactor to become unstable while it was running on a lower-than-usual power level.[9] The resulting explosion, estimated by journalist Patrick Cockburn to be as strong as the blast from

220–441 pounds (100–200 kg) of dynamite, ripped through the unit. Marples adds, "It was the beginning of the worst nuclear accident in history."[10]

The explosion blew the roof off the unit and started 30 fires in the area. Two engineers were killed in the blast. Cockburn writes, "Radiation levels around the blazing ruins of the reactor, where flames were leaping 100 ft [feet, or 30.5 meters] into the air, reached six times the lethal dose for a human being." A team of local firemen tried to put out the fire to prevent it from spreading to another reactor; while the fire was indeed contained, 30 of those firemen died from the radiation. Another 209 people were hospitalized.[11]

While the long-term reaction could not be known immediately, the radioactivity would eventually contaminate 10,000 square miles (25,899.8 square kilometers) of land. In 2000, 14 years after the accident, the Ukrainian health minister said that 3.4 million people had suffered health effects; cases of certain cancers, such as thyroid cancer, were on the rise in Ukraine; and the health ministry had noted a drop in the life spans of people working on the continuing cleanup of Chernobyl.[12]

As Marples notes, the Soviet government initially tried to suppress information about Chernobyl, and reports were released almost two days after the explosion only because of "the discovery of a substantial rise in atmospheric radiation coming from the Soviet Union by the authorities at a nuclear power plant in Sweden. The Soviet media began to issue information only when the Swedes had detected the location of the radiation."[13] At that point, on August 28, buses arrived in Pripyat, the Ukrainian town closest to the reactor site, to evacuate the population. Marples says, "The inhabitants were told they had three hours to leave."[14] They would never be allowed to return.

Chernobyl exposed many flaws in the Soviet system: the inefficiency of the Soviet government, the lack of security and safety measures that had allowed the explosion to occur in the

An aerial view of the Chernobyl nuclear power plant, the site of the world's worst nuclear accident, in April 1986. This photograph, clearly showing the damage to the plant, was made only two or three days after the explosion.

first place, the lag in response time, and the unwillingness of the government to issue factual and accurate information about the disaster. It was a disaster of unimaginable proportions, one that concerned the international community, especially considering the radioactive material had traveled over the western part of the Soviet Union, Eastern Europe, Western Europe,

Northern Europe, and eastern North America. Large areas in Ukraine, Belarus, and Russia were badly contaminated; more than 300,000 people in those areas needed to be evacuated and resettled. Soviet reports initially said that an explosion had caused two deaths, that some areas were being evacuated, and that it was being investigated.

GLASNOST'S INFLUENCE

Around this time, however, the Soviet media was permitted, because of glasnost, more freedom in its reporting. While the government's official stance on Chernobyl attempted to downplay the seriousness of the disaster, journalists investigated and researched the effects of Chernobyl to bring the truth—about the death toll, about the radiation spread, about the regions that were affected—to the Soviet population. As accurate information was offered, and people began to understand the magnitude of the radiation fallout, more and more regions of the USSR (of Belarus, western Ukraine, and more land within Russia) were evacuated. As Marples puts it, "The general attitude among the population was one of panic and disbelief. How could official reports ever be believed again?"[15]

Gorbachev surely expected that glasnost, once set into motion, would grow rapidly, yet he and other members of the Soviet leadership probably were not ready for the fire that glasnost would light. For example, as part of the policy, the government did not abolish censorship, but it did relax restrictions on newspapers as well as the publication of books, pamphlets, and other materials, and on the productions of films that had political content. One of the major issues that these newly liberated venues of information targeted was the corruption of Soviet officials in the past. Marples points to the example of historian Roy Medvedev, who, between November 1988 and February 1989, published his research regarding the actual numbers of Soviet citizens victimized and/or killed during Stalin's reign of terror: The number he published—20 million dead and just as many oppressed—was far greater than any of the official estimates previously provided by the government.[16]

Glasnost also allowed government officials to criticize inefficiencies within the system. One such example came in 1988, Watson writes, when

> government spokesmen admitted that 20 million metric tons of grain were lost each year in the Soviet system owing to the improper storage and transportation. They also admitted that more than 20 billion rubles . . . were lost each year owing to shoddy workmanship and antiquated methods of transportation and storage.[17]

The release of information to the public about the lack of effectiveness and supervision on the part of the government shocked to Soviet citizens. Glasnost also spurred the creation of many new venues of information, such as new newspapers and magazines; one example is a newspaper titled *Glasnost*, "in which common citizens and liberal party activists vented their frustrations against the regime," notes Watson.[18]

The Empire Crumbles

Besides bringing to light past wrongs and current corruption and inefficiency, the policy of glasnost had another effect on the USSR: It contributed to the revolts of the satellite states that wanted to be free of Soviet rule. The challenges to Soviet power within these states would rock the core of the empire that Stalin had forged after World War II.

The Soviet Union was an assembly of several republics, the central one being the republic of Russia. The others included the Baltic states of Estonia, Latvia, and Lithuania; the western states of Ukraine, Belorussia (Belarus), and Moldava; the Transcaucasian states of Georgia, Azerbaijan, and Armenia; and the Central Asian states of Kazakhstan, Uzbekistan, Kyrgyzstan, Tajikistan, and Turkmenistan. While each of these had a different relationship with the Soviet Union, they all shared these common features: The CPSU was the dominating party within their countries and their governments were beholden to the Soviet system. Jeremy Smith notes that several things kept these states in line with CPSU dictates, such as

> repression directed against nationalism, an ideology and education system aimed at promoting the "brotherhood of nations," an economic system which, while failing to promote affluence, delivered a certain level of comfort and job security from the 1960s onwards and the latitude allowed to the national republics in certain spheres.[1]

AN EXCERPT FROM *PERESTROIKA,* BY MIKHAIL GORBACHEV

Perestroika was meant to be a sequence of smaller reforms that would lead to an improved standard of living for the Soviet people. In his 1987 book *Perestroika: New Thinking for Our Country and the World,* Gorbachev outlined some of his thoughts for perestroika, including its hoped-for effects:

> Perestroika is the all-round intensification of the Soviet economy, the revival and development of the principles of democratic centralism in running the national economy, the universal introduction of economic methods, the renunciation of management by injunction and by administrative methods, and the overall encouragement of innovation and socialist enterprise. . . .
>
> Perestroika means priority development of the social sphere aimed at ever better satisfaction of Soviet people's requirements for good living and working conditions, for good rest and recreation, education and health care. It

The USSR also exercised extreme influence in the satellite Eastern European states of Poland, Hungary, Czechoslovakia, East Germany, Bulgaria, and Romania. These client states fell within the Soviets' sphere of influence, as they had Communist regimes that also took their direction from the CPSU. As client states, they received benefits from the USSR such as weapons and cheap gas prices in exchange for their loyalty to the CPSU.

The policy of glasnost helped foster nationalist independent movements in the Soviet republics as well as the client states. Since the majority of the citizens of these states were ethnically not Russian, glasnost helped foster a sense of identity

means unceasing concern for cultural and spiritual wealth, for the culture of every individual and society as a whole.

Perestroika means the elimination from society of the distortions of socialist ethics, the consistent implementation of the principles of social justice. It means the unity of words and deeds, rights and duties. It is the elevation of honest, highly-qualified labor, the overcoming of leveling tendencies in pay and consumerism.

This is how we see Perestroika today. This is how we see our tasks, and the substance and content of our work for the forthcoming period. It is difficult to say how long that period will take. Of course, it will be much more than two or three years. We are ready for serious, strenuous and tedious work to ensure that our country reaches new heights by the end of the twentieth century. . . .

I can say that the end result of Perestroika is clear to us. It is a thorough renewal of every aspect of Soviet life; it is giving socialism the most progressive forms of social organizations; it is the fullest exposure of the humanist nature of our social system in its crucial aspects—economic, social, political and moral.*

* From *Perestroika: New Thinking for Our Country and the World*, by Mikhail Gorbachev, quoted in David Marples, p. 116.

and solidarity among them according to their own language, culture, and political thoughts. Also, because glasnost allowed information to circulate more freely, organizing could take place in a more open environment. Much of the organizing, of course, focused on overthrowing the local Communist regimes, as dissidents, suppressed for so long, were now able to express themselves without fear of punishment.

REFORMS AND REBELLION WITHIN THE REPUBLICS

In many of the Baltic states, independence movements against the USSR formed as a result of Gorbachev's policies of perestroika and glasnost. In 1900, an anti-Communist group had been formed in Lithuania, composed of citizens committed to a Lithuania independent of the USSR. On December 20, 1989, the Lithuanian Communist Party voted overwhelmingly to become independent of Moscow. Because Lithuania was the first of the Soviet republics to declare its independence (in March 1990), Gorbachev decided to take drastic measures to prevent the independence movement from spreading. In January 1991, Gorbachev sent troops into the republic to prevent it from seceding from the union. Thirteen people died, but the military invasion did not succeed in preventing Lithuanians from breaking away from the USSR.

In the spring of 1989, an independence movement emerged in the republic of Georgia, which had become part of the USSR in the 1920s and had been Stalin's homeland. On April 4, a nonviolent protest led by the Independence Committee of Georgia resulted in tens of thousand of people peacefully demonstrating before government offices in Tbilisi, the Georgian capital. The demonstration called for a secession of Georgia from the USSR and an end to Soviet influence. Five days later, on April 9, Soviet troops broke up the demonstration, resulting in the deaths of 20 people. The massacre only fueled the Georgian quest for independence. The Supreme Council of the Republic of Georgia proclaimed independence from the Soviet Union, and it was made official in March 1991. At that point, it was clear that the USSR was falling apart.

CLIENT STATES REJECT COMMUNISM

The succession of demonstrations against the CPSU and Communist rule in general occurred rapidly in the late 1980s. William Watson writes, "A broad-based anti-Soviet movement began in all the Warsaw Pact countries in October 1989, and Gorbachev allowed it to grow."[2] Part of his refusal to quash these movements included Gorbachev's reversal of the so-called Brezhnev Doctrine, which had been in effect since the late 1960s, following the Soviet invasion of Czechoslovakia in August 1968. During his tenure, Brezhnev had stated that the USSR would use force to keep its client states in line with party thinking. Gorbachev realized that military interference in the affairs of these states was costly to the USSR, whose economy was already flailing; he also stated that imposing force was an incorrect action. Furthermore, the benefits that these client states received from the USSR had already proved to be a drain on the Soviet economy, so if they wanted to be liberated from their obligations to the USSR, Gorbachev welcomed that but he hoped that they would willingly retain socialism as their governmental system.

In exchange for this greater independence, Gorbachev wanted the Communist parties in these client states to work hard to win the support of their people, without depending on the Soviet military to back them up. According to Longworth, many objected to Gorbachev's approach: "To those who argued that democracy threatened solidarity, Gorbachev retorted that 'a plurality of views cannot be an obstacle to unity of action.'"[3] To entice the governments of these states to embrace the idea of reformed socialism, Gorbachev implemented free-market reforms in January 1989; the client states would now pay regular prices for Soviet-produced goods and services, which in turn freed these states from their financial (and political) obligations to Moscow.

Such enticements, however, did not work. In many of the client states, the local Communist parties saw their power steadily erode. Communist officials, such as Erich Honeker of East Germany, were thrown out of office and new governments replaced the old regimes. Gorbachev "had hoped for an orderly transition from authoritarian Communism in the countries of the Bloc but . . . the reformed socialism that he promoted was rejected and, rather than the gradualism which he envisaged, change came in a rush."[4] In November 1989 alone, the Communist regimes of Bulgaria, Czechoslovakia, and Hungary were replaced with new governments.

On November 9, 1989, shortly after the ousting of Honecher, people began to tear down the Berlin Wall. President Reagan's words—"Mr. Gorbachev, tear down this wall!"—uttered in June 1987, had actually been a prophecy (even though it was Gorbachev's relaxed policies that allowed the Berlin Wall to be torn down by those who opposed Soviet rule).

At midnight, the Communist government of East Germany, facing widespread protests that had begun in September, allowed the gates of the Berlin Wall to be opened. Throngs of people on both sides of the wall poured through, some greeting relatives and friends from whom they had been separated for decades. It was not long before the wall came under attack by the crowd, as jubilant East and West Berliners climbed atop the structure and began tearing it apart. They used sledgehammers to smash it, knives and rocks to chip away at the mortar, anything they could find to bring down the 28-mile (45-km) barrier that had divided them as a people physically and culturally. While the imposing structure fell apart, slowly but steadily, people celebrated, laughing and crying, stunned that this symbol of Communism was literally crumbling before their eyes. It was amazing to think that anyone attempting to bridge that same wall just a week earlier would have been shot by East German guards. (It is estimated

Jubilant East and West Germans celebrate the fall of the Berlin Wall in November 1989.

that more than 100 people had been killed in the previous three decades while trying to escape from East Berlin to the western part of the city.) Later, as the celebrations escalated, cranes and construction crews arrived to attack the wall more aggressively, while spectators hurried to take away a chunk of cement as a memento of the historic occasion.

Around the world, news of the fall of the Berlin Wall drew cheers and renewed hope. Foreign leaders watched in fascination as the symbol of the iron curtain tumbled; people around the world wondered what this event, which had been so unthinkable, meant for the fate of the Soviet Union. Concerts and galas were held in many European cities to celebrate the fall, as German leaders began talks about how to reunite

Germany. (The official reunification of East and West Germany took place one year later, on October 3, 1990.)

Of all the people watching the fall of the Berlin Wall, perhaps none were more interested and inspired than the citizens of other Soviet client states. Taking their cue from the East Germans, other Eastern European countries began to oust their governments and reform their political systems. This process was mostly a peaceful one, except in Romania, where Nicolae Ceauşescu, the Communist leader, and his wife were executed after his government was overthrown in December 1989. As Watson explains, "That December, the world watched in awe as Communism was repudiated in each of the Warsaw Pact countries. Almost every former client state underwent a transitional period in which Communist reformers or non-Communists made the change from Soviet client to free state."[5]

What did this mean for Mikhail Gorbachev? Marples notes, "In a period of euphoria in Eastern Europe, Gorbachev's reputation was high, not as the architect for change, but because he adopted the role, on behalf of the Soviet Union, as a bystander."[6] Indeed, Gorbachev was quite popular during this period all over the world, except in his own country.

WITHDRAWAL FROM AFGHANISTAN

The Soviet invasion of Afghanistan, begun in 1979, had been successful only at first. The initial invasion was strong and aggressive, but over time, the Red Army began to encounter obstacles. As Gorbachev's policy of glasnost permitted people more freedom to speak without punishment, the unpopularity of the war in Afghanistan became ever more apparent. For example, Andrei Sakharov, whom Gorbachev had released from exile in a gesture of openness, became a vocal critic of the Soviet Union's military presence. Jeremy Smith writes, "It soon became clear that the duration and scale of this intervention would be much greater than anticipated. The war in Afghanistan was not only a drain on manpower and [on]

Soviet mechanized and infantry divisions near the Afghan-Soviet border during the withdrawal from Afghanistan in February 1989.

finances, it was turning into a national humiliation comparable with the earlier US involvement in Vietnam."[7] The calls upon Gorbachev to end the war grew louder; after all, critics argued, Gorbachev had been so willing to break with the old Soviet-style of governing and with other Brezhnev policies, why not end the war Brezhnev had rashly started?

Gorbachev finally took action and, on July 20, 1987, the withdrawal of Soviet troops from the country was announced. By February 15, 1989, all Soviet troops were out of the war-torn nation, which had seen an estimated one million Afghanis killed. In the process of withdrawing, the Soviet government released information regarding the numbers of its own losses: 13,310 soldiers had died and 35,478 had been wounded. While these numbers were high, the real count was actually higher, as David Marples points out, because "they omitted disease and drug addiction victims."[8]

While the withdrawal from Afghanistan was necessary to stop the drain it was causing on the Soviet economy and military, the decision still proved unpopular in some circles because it was, as Marples notes, "an admission of failure, and one unlikely to appease the families of Soviet soldiers who had died in the war."[9] It did, however, improve morale at home and the level of confidence Western governments had in the reforming Soviet administration. The withdrawal was a major signal from Gorbachev to the world that the Soviet Union was willing to work toward peaceful relations.

Unfortunately for Gorbachev, things were spiraling out of his control.

The August Coup

Boris Yeltsin had been a rising star in the Communist Party of the Soviet Union—elected to the Supreme Soviet, then to the Central Committee, and then as a candidate member of the Politburo—until 1988, when he fell out of favor with the party's leadership. Some leaders, such as Yegor Ligachev, accused him of trying to divide the party; by gaining popularity with the reforms he made on a local level in Moscow, Yeltsin was allegedly currying disfavor in the CPSU because it could not seem to implement the same reforms on a national level.

Yeltsin had indeed been publicly critical of the CPSU. At the October 1987 Central Committee Plenum, he issued a critique of Gorbachev's policy of perestroika. The archives of that plenum recorded the attacks made upon Yeltsin; for example, First Party Secretary of Ukraine Volodymyr Shcherbytsky dismissed Yeltsin's speech: "Now what is it that Comrade Yeltsyn [*sic*] disagrees with? Either he disagrees in substance with the line toward *perestroika* and the evaluation of the state of affairs and the immediate tasks as outlined in this report. Or perhaps he is afraid of the difficulties to come." Shcherbytsky also claimed Yeltsin's comments were "politically immature" and "an ill-conceived step taken under some wrong impression."[1] The party leaders wanted to bring Yeltsin down quickly from his position before he eroded their authority any further. According to Marples, in Yeltsin's memoir, the Soviet leader described the day in November 1987 when he was dragged before the party's leadership, despite having recently suffered a heart attack, and dismissed from his position as the Moscow party secretary:

> What do you call it when a person is murdered with words? Because what followed was like a real murder. After all, I could have been dismissed in a sentence or two, then and there, at the plenum. But no; they had to enjoy the whole process of public betrayal, when comrades who had been working alongside me for two years, without the slightest sign of discord in our relations, suddenly began to say things that to this day my mind refuses to absorb.[2]

Watson writes that despite his dismissal, Yeltsin was "so popular with the public that he could not be denied power altogether. In the era of glasnost, the party did not have the same options to crush dissent as it had in earlier years."[3] He was appointed minister of the building industry, remained on the Central Committee, and was named an attendee of the party conference. During that conference, Yeltsin continued to stoke the fire of reform and even carried it to a national level by portraying himself as an agent of change.

In late November 1988, bowing to reform pressures, the Supreme Soviet was dissolved and a new body, the Congress of People's Deputies, put in its place. For the first time in Soviet history, an election would not be limited only to candidates

BORIS YELTSIN

Boris Nikolayevich Yeltsin was born on February 1, 1931 in Butka, a village in the mountainous Sverdlovsk region of northern Russia. Like Gorbachev's family, Yeltsin's was of humble origins. His father was a construction worker—the same profession his son later used to rise up through the ranks of the political system. Boris Yeltsin studied civil engineering at the Kirov Urals Polytechnical Institute, graduating in 1955, and was hired soon after to work on a government construction project. He joined the Communist Party in 1961 and quickly gained friends through his magnanimous personality. He was also success- ful in the construction trade and was continually promoted to higher positions.

In 1974, Yeltsin was elected to the Supreme Soviet. Two years later, he was appointed regional first secretary of the Sverdlovsk regional party. In 1981, he was appointed to the Central Committee. When Gorbachev was elected general secretary in 1985, Yeltsin advocated Gorbachev's reform ideas. In return, Gorbachev named him first secre- tary of Moscow's Communist Party organization, known as the *gorkom*. William Watson says the gorkom's past lead- ers exploited it for financial gain and power. Yeltsin was charged by Gorbachev with reforming it.

In Moscow, Yeltsin founded a platform for his own political rise. He became known as an enemy of the appa- ratchikis, a man who did not tolerate corruption in any form. Watson writes that Yeltsin "gave up his own private car and dacha (summer cottage) and urged others to do the same. He preferred to take public transportation such as the subway or bus to emphasize that it was time for

(continues)

(continued)

austerity measures within the party in order to improve the country's economy."* These measures, and others, made him seem like one of the people.

As Yeltsin's popularity was increasing, Gorbachev's was declining. When Yeltsin became a candidate member of the Politburo in 1986, many party members suspicious of his attacks on the party tried to oust him from his position. Yeltsin suffered a heart attack from the stress, but four days after the attack, he was brought before party officials to defend himself against charges that he was intentionally trying to divide the party. According to Marples, Yeltsin recalled that day in his 1990 memoir, *Against the Grain*:

> On the morning of November 11, the telephone rang on my special Kremlin line. . . . It was Gorbachev and he spoke as if he were calling me not in the hospital but at my dacha. In a calm voice he said: "You must come and see me for a short while, Boris Nikolayevich. After that, perhaps we will go and attend the plenum of the Moscow City Committee

from the Communist Party. When the elections were held in March 1989, the party, as expected, fared poorly. The big winner, however, was Boris Yeltsin, who won 89 percent of the vote in his bid to be elected as the Moscow delegate to the Congress, easily defeating his opponent, a candidate from the CPSU. Those same elections, which drew 89.8 percent of the electorate in general, threw out the highest-ranking people in the CPSU, sweeping new voices into office to replace them.[4]

Jeremy Smith notes that Yeltsin, ever a savvy politician, "seized the opportunity of the elections to the Congress of People's Deputies in 1989 to launch a remarkable comeback."[5]

together." I said I couldn't come because I was I [in] bed
and the doctors wouldn't let me get up. . . . In all my life
I had never heard of anyone, whether a worker or a man-
ager, being dragged out of a hospital bed to be dismissed.
It is simply unheard of . . . However much Gorbachev may
have disliked me, to act like that was inhuman and immoral. . . . I was thus barely conscious when I appeared at the
Politburo. I was in the same condition when I arrived at the
plenum of the City Committee.**

Yeltsin lost his position as leader of the gorkom and
later removed from his candidate membership in the
Politburo. Gorbachev did nothing to defend Yeltsin, causing an enormous rift between the two men that would
later exacerbate the tenuous political situation—and help
bring about the kind of radical change the party leaders
feared most.

---

* William E. Watson, *The Collapse of the Soviet Union*. Westport,
Conn.: Greenwood Press, 1998. p. 80.
** David R. Marples. *The Collapse of the Soviet Union: 1981-
1991*. New York: Pearson Longman, 2004, p. 120.

In May 1990, having already gained a seat in the Congress, he
was elected its chairman. He quit the Communist Party two
months later. In June 1990, he pushed the Congress to declare
that the republic of Russia was independent from the USSR;
whenever the USSR issued policies or declared laws that con-
flicted with the policies and laws of Russia, the Russian republic
was not obligated to accede to the USSR. "This sovereignty,"
notes Jeremy Smith, "was not recognized by Gorbachev and
was against the terms of the Soviet constitution."[6]
In June 1991, Yeltsin was elected the president of the Russian
Republic, winning 57 percent of the vote. From this position,

Russian leaders Mikhail Gorbachev, right, and Boris Yeltsin in 1991, during the dying days of the Soviet Union.

Yeltsin became the voice for the other republics, which also wanted to be independent from the USSR. By promising to support the independence of other republics, he increased his popular support in Russia. He also forged an alliance with the long-suppressed Russian Orthodox Church and its leadership, which helped to expand his base of support. Smith writes that Yeltsin put forth the idea that "Russia would be politically and economically more stable if it broke or weakened its ties with the other republics."[7] For the first time, it seemed possible that the integrity of the Soviet Union was in danger of falling apart.

What had started as a move to release the satellite states from CPSU control now turned internal: Republics within the Soviet Union wanted more freedom as well. They had a charismatic and vocal advocate in Yeltsin, for whom 200,000

Russians marched in Moscow in a show of support in March 1991. His popularity was undermining Gorbachev and the core of power in the Soviet Union—and neither the CPSU nor Gorbachev knew how to stop it.

COUP D'ETAT

Mikhail Gorbachev knew he had to deal with the problem of Boris Yeltsin—and quickly. As general secretary, Gorbachev had enjoyed many successes, such as popularity around the world and an end to the war in Afghanistan, but his policies of glasnost and perestroika had also exposed the Soviet Union's weak underbelly: The Soviet empire had essentially collapsed with the independence of the Eastern European client states, and now, because of Yeltsin, the republics within the Soviet Union were also calling for independence from the USSR.

In March 1991, a referendum was held to gauge whether there was popular support for preserving the Soviet Union. The question, crafted by Gorbachev himself, was phrased this way: "Do you think that it is necessary to preserve the Union of Soviet Socialist Republics as a renewed federation of equal and sovereign republics in which the rights and freedoms of each citizen, regardless of ethnic origin, will be fully guaranteed?" He asked for a simple "yes" or "no" answer.[8] Although the referendum passed with a majority showing support for keeping the union intact, it was still obvious that people felt change was needed, and quickly.

In response to the referendum, Gorbachev proposed the New Union Treaty, which laid out the principles that would allow the republics to remain anchored to the USSR but have more political leverage and freedom. In April, Boris Yeltsin—as well as the leaders of the other republics of the USSR—agreed with the idea, which helped Gorbachev to win support for it. It was due to be signed on August 20, 1991. A few days before the signing, Gorbachev retired to his private residence in Foros, located in the Crimea, to finalize the document.

What happened in those few days between August 18 and 21 is still debated. It is known that a coup to oust Gorbachev from power was attempted. The group called itself the State

STATE OF EMERGENCY: AUGUST 20, 1991

The following statement was issued on August 20, 1991 by the leaders of the State Emergency Committee to rally support for their coup d'etat. In their appeal, excerpted below, the committee tried to steer support of the population away from reform leaders, whom they portrayed as lawbreakers trying to undermine the Soviet system:

Fellow countrymen! Citizens of the Soviet Union!

At this grave, critical hour for the fate of the fatherland and of our peoples, we appeal to you! A mortal danger threatens our great homeland! For a number of reasons, the policy of reforms begun at the initiative of MS Gorbachev and conceived of as a means of ensuring the dynamic development of the country and democratization of the life of society had reached an impasse. The initial enthusiasm and hopes have given way to unbelief, apathy and despair. The authorities at all levels have lost the trust of the population. In the life of society, political intrigue has supplanted concern for the fate of the fatherland and the citizen. Malicious mocking of all state institutions is being propagated. In essence, the country had become ungovernable. . . .

The people should decide what the social system should be like, but they are being deprived of this right.

Instead of showing concern for the security and well-being of every citizen and of society as a whole, the peo-

Emergency Committee, and the leaders of the August Putsch, or August Coup, acted on August 18. According to Jeremy Smith, the members of the Committee included such high

ple who have acquired power frequently use it for interests that are alien to the people, as a means of unscrupulous self-assertion. The streams of words and mountains of statements and promises only underscore the scanty and wretched nature of their practical deeds. The inflation of power, more frightening than any other kinds of inflation, is destroying our state and society. Every citizen feels growing uncertainty about tomorrow and deep concern for the future of his or her children. . . .

For many years, we have heard from all sides incantations about commitment to the interests of the individual, to concern for his rights and social safeguards. But in fact people have been humiliated, their real rights and possibilities have been infringed, and they have been driven to despair. All the democratic institutions created through the expression of the people's will are losing their authority and effectiveness before our very eyes. This is the result of purposeful actions by those who, blatantly flouting the USSR Basic Law, are staging an unconstitutional coup, to all intents and purposes, and longing for unbridled personal dictatorship. Prefectures, mayoralties and other unlawful structures are increasingly supplanting, in an unauthorized way, the Soviets that have been elected by the people. . . .

We call on all citizens of the Soviet Union to recognize their duty to the homeland and provide every kind of support to the State Committee for the State of Emergency in the USSR and to efforts to bring the country out of crisis.*

* Richard Sakwa. *The Rise and Fall of the Soviet Union: 1917-1991*. New York: Routledge, 1991, pp. 479-482.

officials as Gennady Yanayev (Gorbachev's vice president), Vladimir Kryuchkov (the head of the KGB), Valentin Pavlov (the prime minister), Dmitri Yazov and Boris Pugo (the ministers of defense and the interior), and Valeri Boldin (Gorbachev's trusted chief of staff).[9] A representative of this committee went before Gorbachev, in his residence, and requested that he approve a state of emergency plan. Gorbachev refused.

The committee responded by placing him under house arrest, and the next day, it seized control of all the media, including newspapers and radio and television stations. Smith writes that "the Committee announced that Gorbachev was sick and Yanayev was assuming his powers. . . . They also announced a six month state of emergency, a ban on strikes, demonstrations, opposition political activities, and the subordination of all levels of government to the Committee."[10] Because the committee's members also included important and high-ranking military officials, the force behind their bold statement was palpable. Many oppositionist leaders were promptly arrested, and the military's tanks soon began patrolling the streets of Moscow to prevent demonstrations or trouble.

What were the committee's aims? Smith surmises that the coup's leaders wanted to prevent Gorbachev from signing the New Union Treaty, which they viewed as a threat to the integrity of the USSR. "One interpretation," Smith writes, "is that the coup organizers, who included a number of people close to Gorbachev, did not intend to overthrow him, but rather to put pressure on him and encourage him to stand up to Yeltsin and other opponents without fear."[11] According to Sakwa, Boris Yeltsin proclaimed: "The date—this is absolutely clear—was chosen not at random: the last day before the signing of the new Union Treaty," which he explains would have ended the power of the CPSU, thus prompting the party's highest officials to preserve the authority of the party.[12]

What the members of the State Emergency Committee did not count on was Boris Yeltsin. For some reason, Yeltsin

Russian President Boris Yeltsin, atop a tank, reads from a prepared speech to demonstrators in front of the Soviet parliament in Moscow on August 19, 1991.

had not been arrested, although it seems that he was one of the persons the committee had on its list. He and many of his supporters, including Eduard Shevardnadze and the widow of Andrei Sakharov, gathered in front of the parliamentary building in Moscow to protest the coup. The protest grew to include many thousands of angry Russians, and similar demonstrations were organized throughout the USSR.

Yeltsin's appeal to end the coup and restore Gorbachev to power was not surprising, despite the fact that the two men were political enemies. Yeltsin sensed that a successful coup by the State Emergency Committee would put an end to all his efforts to gain more freedom for the Russian republic, that it was actually a return to the old, authoritarian system of government.

On August 19, Yeltsin made a dramatic appearance at the parliament building, walking up to a tank that did not dare fire at him and entered into the building. Sakwa writes that, from there, Yeltsin made the following statement:

On the night of 18 to 19 August 1991 the legally elected president of the country was removed from power. Whatever reasons might be given to justify this removal, we are dealing with a right-wing, reactionary and anti-constitutional group.

Notwithstanding all the trials and difficulties the people of our country are experiencing, the democratic process in the country is becoming ever deeper and is becoming irreversible. The peoples of Russia are becoming masters of their own fate. . . .

Such a development aroused the animosity of reactionary forces and provoked them to try to solve the most complicated political and economic problems by the use of force. . . .

We have always considered that the use of force to solve political and economic problems is unacceptable. It discredits the USSR in the eyes of the world and undermines our prestige in the international community, returning us to the Cold War era and the isolation of the Soviet Union from the international community.

We are forced to declare unlawful this so-called committee together with all its decisions and resolutions.[13]

Yeltsin also demanded that Gorbachev be allowed to come out from under house arrest and address the people of the USSR. He furthermore called for a general strike to protest the coup, and called upon the military not to cooperate with its leaders. In fact, the military seemed reluctant to act against the demonstrators. While the committee leadership ordered that the demonstrations be brought swiftly under control, the military took a passive role. Smith explains that, because of Yeltsin's involvement and the protest that he helped launch, the committee's attempt to present the coup as a choice between Gorbachev's ineffectiveness and Yanayev's leadership failed; instead, the two opposing sides became "democracy" versus "authoritarian rule," as well as "freedom" and "the old days of the Gulag and the KGB"—which nobody wanted to see return, not even the military.[14]

On August 21, Yazov, the minister of defense, abandoned the committee and ordered the military action to stop. The coup was officially over when most of the committee members were arrested and the released Gorbachev was flown back to Moscow, but the collapse of the Soviet Union came quickly after the failed August Putsch.

THE SWIFT END

On August 24, 1991, just a few days after the attempted coup, Gorbachev resigned as the general secretary of the Communist Party of the Soviet Union. He also dissolved the Central Committee. Most of the government's power was quickly passing into the hands of the Russian Republic. On September 6, the Soviet Union recognized the independence of the Warsaw Pact states, which were clamoring to declare themselves sovereign of the USSR. In Moscow, at the Kremlin, the red hammer-and-sickle Soviet flag was flown alongside the official tricolor flag of the Russian Republic for the first time, signaling a ceding of power from Gorbachev to Yeltsin.

In the meantime, a new union was secretly being formed behind Mikhail Gorbachev's back: the leaders of Russia, Ukraine, and Belarus were laying the groundwork for the Commonwealth of Independent States (CIS) as a replacement for the USSR. Yeltsin, Ukrainian President Leonid Kravchuk, and Belarusian President Stanislav Shushkevich held secret talks and negotiations at a hunting lodge in Belarus. The CIS, as they envisioned it, would be a loose confederation of the Soviet republics. Headquartered in Minsk, Belarus, the CIS would be loose enough to allow for democracy and independence for all members, but would regulate trade, economic issues, and border concerns of the republics.

On December 8, the maneuverings of Yeltsin, Kravchuk, and Shushkevich were made public; on that day, they announced that the USSR "as a subject of international and geopolitical reality no longer exists." They further revealed the establishment of the CIS, and most other republics decided to join the new union. The formation of the CIS was the final blow to any possibility of preserving the USSR. To most, it was now clear that Boris Yeltsin had finally won the power struggle. In fact, the creation of the CIS left Mikhail Gorbachev without an entity over which to govern. He became, in effect, jobless. Serge Schmemann, writing in the *New York Times*, said, "Now, the man who set out almost seven years earlier to reform the world's biggest empire finds himself on the verge of being swept aside by the very forces he set loose."[15]

On December 25, in a 10-minute speech, Mikhail Gorbachev shook the world by announcing his resignation from the Soviet presidency and the impending dissolution of the USSR. That night, the Russian flag replaced the flag of the USSR, which was taken down from atop the Kremlin in Moscow. On December 26, the main chamber of the Soviet Supreme officially recognized the dissolution of the USSR. The union would be replaced by 15 separate countries. On December 31, 1991, all institutions of the USSR ceased to exist. All federal government power passed to the Russian Republic and into the hands of its president, Boris Yeltsin, including the USSR's seat at the United Nations.

The 74-year history of the USSR had come to a shockingly rapid and peaceful end.

After the Fall

Although some nations with Communist regimes, such as Vietnam, North Korea, and Cuba, were despondent about the collapse of the Soviet Union and feared for the viability of their own regimes, most of the world celebrated the end of the Soviet empire and the freedom of its republics.

Because the United States had lost its major opponent on the world's political stage, it was clear that America was now the leader in world affairs. (In fact, at the Arab-Israeli peace talks that were taking place at the time, the Soviet Union had a diminished role, making America's lead all the more obvious.) The Western world in general was happy that the Soviet system was now gone, and the Cold War—with its ever-present threat of nuclear war—was finally over. To many looking in from the outside, it appeared that the Soviet Union suddenly and dramatically came apart at the seams. To those inside, and particularly those within the higher echelons of the party, the Soviet Union had been dying for a long time.

How did this happen? While historians agree that Mikhail Gorbachev had wanted only to reform the USSR and had not intended the union to collapse, there is not a simple answer to this question. For example, historian Philip Longworth argues that Gorbachev attempted political reform, such as perestroika and glasnost, but not economic reform, which the USSR sorely needed.[1] Yet Jeremy Smith offers a contrasting perspective, arguing that Gorbachev's mistake was trying to implement political and economic reform at the same time.

While people outside the former USSR were generally happy at the stunning turn of events, within the republics, fear and panic set in almost immediately. Todd Brewster wrote in *Life* a month after the collapse, "History shows us that empires don't die tidy deaths and do not go gentle into that good night."[2] Brewster also noted:

> The dizzying pace of change—Communist party headquarters padlocked, the KGB gutted and stripped of power—produced more panic than joy, with ominous questions hanging like so many dark clouds. Who had controlled the nuclear trigger during the coup? . . . What would become of the 5,000 warheads positioned in the outlying republics once they broke with Moscow?[3]

Other questions concerned the rising prices for basic needs, such as bread and milk. The wheat harvest had come in, for example, 30 percent lower than normal, and long lines formed at state-operated distribution centers. Richard Ericson of the Harriman Institute warned of "the largest man-made disaster the world has ever seen."[4] U.S. Secretary of State James Baker described the plight of former Soviet citizens as "their

DISSOLUTION OF SOVIET UNION

In this speech Mikhail Gorbachev announced his resignation as president and the dissolution of the USSR:

Dear compatriots, fellow citizens, as a result of the newly formed situation, . . . I cease my activities in the post of the U.S.S.R. president. I am taking this decision out of considerations based on principle. I have firmly stood for independence, self-rule of nations, for the sovereignty of the republics, but at the same time for preservation of the union state, the unity of the country. . . .

Addressing you for the last time in the capacity of president of the U.S.S.R., I consider it necessary to express my evaluation of the road we have traveled since 1985, especially as there are a lot of contradictory, superficial and subjective judgments on that matter.

Fate had it that when I found myself at the head of the state it was already clear that all was not well in the country. There is plenty of everything: land, oil and gas, other natural riches, and God gave us lots of intelligence and talent, yet we lived much worse than developed countries and keep falling behind them more and more.

The reason could already be seen: The society was suffocating in the vise of the command-bureaucratic system, doomed to serve ideology and bear the terrible burden of the arms race. It had reached the limit of its possibilities. All attempts at partial reform, and there had been many, had suffered defeat, one after another. The country was losing perspective. We could not go on living like that. Everything had to be changed radically.

The process of renovating the country and radical changes in the world turned out to be far more compli-

(continues)

(continued)

cated than could be expected. However, what has been done ought to be given its due. This society acquired freedom, liberated itself politically and spiritually, and this is the foremost achievement which we have not yet understood completely, because we have not learned to use freedom.

However, work of historic significance has been accomplished. The totalitarian system which deprived the country of an opportunity to become successful and prosperous long ago has been eliminated. A breakthrough has been achieved on the way to democratic changes. Free elections, freedom of the press, religious freedoms, representative organs of power, a multiparty (system) became a reality; human rights are recognized as the supreme principle. . . .

We live in a new world. The Cold War has ended, the arms race has stopped, as has the insane militarization which mutilated our economy, public psyche and morals. The threat of a world war has been removed. Once again I want to stress that on my part everything was done during the transition period to preserve reliable control of the nuclear weapons.

We opened ourselves to the world, gave up interference into other people's affairs, the use of troops beyond the borders of the country, and trust, solidarity and respect came in response.

hour of despair" and encouraged Western nations to help ease the financial crisis.[5]

YELTSIN: A FAILED REFORMER?

If many Russians looked to their new president, Boris Yeltsin, to save them in this time of crisis following the collapse, to act

The nations and peoples of this country gained real freedom to choose the way of their self-determination. The search for a democratic reformation of the multinational state brought us to the threshold of concluding a new Union Treaty. All these changes demanded immense strain. They were carried out with sharp struggle, with growing resistance from the old, the obsolete forces.

The old system collapsed before the new one had time to begin working, and the crisis in the society became even more acute.

The August coup brought the general crisis to its ultimate limit. The most damaging thing about this crisis is the breakup of the statehood. And today I am worried by our people's loss of the citizenship of a great country. The consequences may turn out to be very hard for everyone.

I am leaving my post with apprehension, but also with hope, with faith in you, your wisdom and force of spirit. We are the heirs of a great civilization, and its rebirth into a new, modern and dignified life now depends on one and all.

Some mistakes could surely have been avoided, many things could have been done better, but I am convinced that sooner or later our common efforts will bear fruit, our nations will live in a prosperous and democratic society.

I wish all the best to all of you.*

---

* "Gorbachev Speech, Dissolving the Soviet Union (USSR): Christmas 1991." http://www.publicpurpose.com/lib-gorb 911225.htm.

the hero as he had been during the struggle for independence, they were sorely disappointed. Since the vast majority of Russian industries were state-owned, Yeltsin set about privatizing the Russian economy. By most accounts the transition was handled sloppily and the Russian people suffered for it. A small group of Russian tycoons, known by the mid-1990s as the "oligarchs," were the recipients of the lion's share of the state's assets. Controlling interests in energy, finance, industry, telecommunications, and the media were effectively given away to this select few as average Russians watched their standard of living decrease to shocking levels during the Yeltsin presidency. Many wished for the security that the Soviet Union had provided them in the past.

Between 1994 and 1996, Yeltsin embroiled Russia in a war against Chechnya, a small section of the republic that had declared its sovereignty in 1993. The conflict was so brutal that most Russians opposed it, and Yeltsin was forced to order a cease-fire two years later. Chechnyan rebels launched attacks within Russia, however, and in August 1999, Russia again invaded Chechnya and reseized the area as part of its borders, causing Chechnyan militants to escalate their attacks. The prolonged conflict with Russia was deeply unpopular and many Russians felt that Yeltsin could have handled it more decisively.

Furthermore, Yeltsin seemed to stir media controversies almost regularly, especially in 1993, when he appeared before the Russian congress seemingly drunk. He also had a habit of taking long, unannounced vacations, where reports whispered that he went on drinking and partying binges. He also displayed his anger and stubbornness at embarrassing times; for example, he once refused to greet former U.S. President Richard Nixon, who was visiting Russia, which caused diplomatic embarrassment.

Following his 1987 heart attack, Yeltsin suffered from many health problems. During his presidency, he had to undergo a quintuple bypass operation because of heart blockages. He reportedly suffered from liver problems due, allegedly, to his alcohol addiction, although other sources said he suffered from a neurological disorder. *Time* stated simply, "There is clearly a physical change in a politician who cemented his power in 1991 by boldly scrambling atop a tank outside the besieged White House."[6]

Yeltsin was also plagued by charges of corruption. In 1999, it was alleged that he had several foreign bank accounts containing millions of dollars, and that he was involved in money laundering. On December 31, 1999, rather than deliver his usual New Year's address via television, Yeltsin stunned Russians by immediately resigning before his term had expired: "I am stepping down ahead of term. I understand that I must do it and Russia must enter the new millennium with new politicians, with new faces, with new intelligent, strong, energetic people, and we who have been in power for many years must go."

Yeltsin spoke honestly to the Russian people about the fact that his presidency had not lived up to their expectations for a strong nation. In his resignation speech, Yeltsin asked Russians to forgive him for his shortcomings. "Many of our hopes have not come true," he said simply, "because what we thought would be easy turned out to be painfully difficult."

Writing in *Newsweek*, Bill Powell said, "On his last day in office, Yeltsin acknowledged for the first time what is plainly obvious to most of Russia's citizens: his era, which began with such soaring possibility, has declined into a dispiriting mix of economic despair, rampant corruption and war."[7]

Yeltsin was immediately replaced by Vladimir Putin, a former KGB agent who had become prime minister only a few months earlier. Putin served as acting president of Russia for the next three months. One of Putin's first actions as president was to make sure that Yeltsin and his family would never be implicated in any corruption investigations. When presidential elections were held in March 2000, Putin's victory was decisive.

THE PUTIN ERA

As a leader, Putin moved swiftly to solidify his power base and to address major problems. The war in Chechnya was an ongoing source of concern among Russians, and in May 2000, Putin was able to establish direct rule in the region. In 2003, a new constitution in Chechnya allowed the region some degree

Vladimir Putin speaks to the media in Moscow on October 1, 1999. Although wildly popular in Russia, Putin is considered by many observers to be an autocratic leader.

of autonomy, although those Chechnyans who still desire a full separation from Russia now continue their efforts, most visibly in the form of insurgent attacks on Russia.

Because Putin is known to mourn the collapse of the Soviet Union, many world leaders have been wary of him. In 2007, *Time* named him its "Person of the Year" for the way that he managed to improve life for Russians within eight years, mostly due to economic reform: "Putin is, above all, a pragmatist," *Time*'s editors wrote, noting that he helped rebuild the Russian economy based on a free-market system. This was also balanced by his strengthening the role of the government. His goal is to restore the status of Russia as a world leader. "If he succeeds," *Time*'s editors remarked, "Russia will become a political competitor to the U.S. and to rising nations like China and India. It will be one of the great powers of the new world."[8]

In late 2007, Putin announced he would not seek to run for a third presidential term when his second term ended in 2008. He did, however, use his widespread popularity to encourage the election of his protégé, Dmitry Medvedev. After Medvedev's victory, the new president appointed Putin in May 2008 to the post of Russian prime minister, in which he has control over most foreign, domestic, and security issues. Many analysts saw the move as Putin's way of maintaining control over the governmental system he had helped build and strengthen. His continuing influence will likely help define Russia for the foreseeable future and determine whether it will return to its autocratic past or find a new future as a fully democratic society.

CHRONOLOGY

1917 The Bolshevik Revolution establishes Communism in Russia.

1918-1920 The Russian Civil War between Bolsheviks and their rivals ends with a Bolshevik victory and the establishment of the Union of Soviet Socialist Republics (USSR).

1922 Joseph Stalin comes to power in Russia.

1941 Nazi Germany invades the Soviet Union, breaking a previous treaty not to do so; the USSR enters World War II.

TIMELINE

1922
Joseph Stalin comes to power in Russia.

1917
The Bolshevik Revolution establishes Communism in Russia.

1941
Nazi Germany invades the Soviet Union, breaking a previous treaty not to do so; the USSR enters World War II.

1917

1985

1918–1920
The Russian Civil War between Bolsheviks and their rivals ends with a Bolshevik victory and the establishment of the USSR.

1962
The United States and the USSR come close to nuclear war over the placement of Soviet missiles in Cuba, close to the American border.

1985
March Mikhail Gorbachev is elected general secretary of Communist Party of the Soviet Union (CPSU).

1945   Meeting of Great Britain, the United States, and the Soviet Union in Yalta to decide on spheres of influence.

1955   The Warsaw Pact adds several client states to the USSR's sphere of influence.

1962   The United States and the USSR come close to nuclear war over the placement of Soviet missiles in Cuba, close to the American border.

1979   The USSR invades Afghanistan, the beginning of a long and protracted conflict.

1985   March Mikhail Gorbachev is elected general secretary of Communist Party of the Soviet Union (CPSU).

1986
One of the nuclear reactors at Chernobyl, in Ukraine, explodes, causing an unprecedented environmental disaster.

1989
November The Berlin Wall is breached and torn down, symbolizing the unraveling of the USSR's power.

1986

1991

1991
June Boris Yeltsin is elected president of Russia.
August Several leaders of the CPSU, including some that are close to Gorbachev, stage a coup to oust him from power. The coup fails and instead bolsters the popularity of Boris Yeltsin.
December 25 Gorbachev resigns as leader of the Soviet Union.
December 31 The Soviet Union is officially dissolved, breaking up into 15 independent republics.

1985	**December** Boris Yeltsin is appointed by Gorbachev as head of the Communist Party in Moscow.
1986	One of the nuclear reactors at Chernobyl, in Ukraine, explodes, causing an unprecedented environmental disaster.
1987	Yeltsin is ousted from his position for allegedly posing a threat to the integrity of the CPSU.
1989	Elections are held for the newly formed Congress of People's Deputies; Yeltsin regains his political clout in being elected as the Moscow representative. Gorbachev states that the USSR will not interfere in the autonomy of the Warsaw Pact states.
	November The Berlin Wall in Germany is breached and torn down, symbolizing the unraveling of the USSR's power.
1991	**June** Boris Yeltsin is elected president of Russia.
	August Several leaders of the CPSU, including some that are close to Gorbachev, stage a coup to oust him from power. The coup fails and instead bolsters the popularity of Boris Yeltsin.
	December 8 The presidents of Russia, Belarus, and Ukraine secretly meet to outline the formation of the Council of Independent States (CIS) as a replacement for the USSR.
	December 25 Gorbachev resigns as leader of the Soviet Union.
	December 31 The Soviet Union is officially dissolved, breaking up into 15 independent republics.

NOTES

CHAPTER 1

1. Ronald Reagan. "Remarks at the Brandenburg Gate." June 12, 1987. http://www.reagan foundation.org/pdf/Remarks_ on_East_West_RElations_at_ Bradenburg%20Gate_061287. pdf.
2. Reagan, "Remarks."
3. Derek Maus, ed. *Russia*. New York, Greenhaven Press, 2003, p. 14.
4. Ibid., p. 7.
5. Ibid., p. 14.
6. Ibid., p. 14.
7. Leo de Hartog. "Russia Under the 'Mongol Yoke,'" In *Russia*, ed. Derek Maus. New York: Greenhaven Press, 2003, p. 70.
8. Jules Koslow, "Ivan the Terrible and His Oprichnina," In *Russia,* ed. Derek Maus. New York: Greenhaven Press, 2003, p. 87.
9. Koslow, pp. 90–91.

CHAPTER 2

1. D.S. Mirsky. "Peter the Great's Governmental Reforms," In *Russia*, ed. Derek Maus. New York: Greenhaven Press, p. 110.
2. Ibid., p. 110.
3. Ibid., p. 114.
4. James H. Billington. "The Russian Enlightenment," In *Russia*, ed. Derek Maus. New York: Greenhaven Press, 2003, p. 115.
5. Ibid., pp. 115–116.
6. Ibid., p. 121.
7. Ibid., p. 122.

8. Alexander II, "The Emancipation Manifesto," In *Russia*, ed. Derek Maus. New York: Greenhaven Press, 2003, p. 144.
9. "October Manifesto." http:// www.britannica.com/EB checked/topic/424878/October-Manifesto.

CHAPTER 3

1. William E. Watson. *The Collapse of Communism in the Soviet Union*. Westport, Conn.: Greenwood Press, 1998, p. 3.
2. Richard Sakwa. *The Rise and Fall of the Soviet Union: 1917–1991*. New York: Routledge, 1999, p. 6.
3. Ibid., p. 3.
4. Watson, p. 4.
5. Sakwa, p. 11.
6. Ibid., p. 8.
7. Ibid., p. 9.
8. Geoffrey Hosking. "The Two Revolutions of 1917," In *Russia*, ed. Derek Maus. New York: Greenhaven Press, 2003, p. 163.
9. Ibid., pp. 163–164.
10. Sakwa, p. 48.
11. Hosking, p. 166.

CHAPTER 4

1. Evan Mawdsley. "Why the Bolsheviks Won the Russian Civil War." In *Russia*, ed. Derek Maus. New York: Greenhaven Press, 2003, p. 74.
2. Ibid., p. 173.
3. Sakwa, *Rise*, p. 143.

4. Ibid., p. 123.
5. Ibid., p. 125.
6. Ibid., p. 125.
7. Andrei Sinyavsky, "The Effects of the Stalinist Terror," In *Russia*, ed. Derek Maus. New York: Greenhaven Press, 2003, p. 183.
8. Sakwa, p. 199.
9. Sinyavsky, p. 187.
10. Sakwa, p. 218.
11. Ibid., p. 228.
12. Ibid., p. 254.
13. Ibid., p. 256.
14. Ibid., p. 257.
15. Ibid., p. 269.

CHAPTER 5

1. Thomas W. Wolfe. "How Stalin's Actions Helped Start the Cold War," In *Russia*, ed. Derek Maus. New York: Greenhaven Press, 2003, p. 201.
2. Sakwa, *Rise*, p. 289.
3. Winston Churchill. "The Sinews of Peace." March 5, 1946. http://www.hpol.org/churchill/.
4. Philip Longworth, *Russia: The Once and Future Empire from Pre-History to Putin*. New York: St. Martin's Press, 2005, p. 261.
5. Ibid., p. 267.
6. Ibid., p. 267.
7. Watson, *Collapse of Communism*, p. 5.
8. Ibid., p. 20.
9. Ibid., p. 20.
10. Longworth, p. 272.
11. David R. Marples. *The Collapse of the Soviet Union: 1985–1991.*

New York: Pearson Longman, 2004, p. 138.
12. Longworth, p. 299.
13. Jeremy Smith. *The Fall of Soviet Communism: 1985–1991.* New York: Palgrave Macmillan 2005, p. 14
14. Longworth, p. 299.
15. Smith, p. 36.
16. Marples, p. 17.
17. Watson, pp. 28–29.
18. Smith, p. 11.
19. Watson, p. 31.

CHAPTER 6

1. Watson, *Collapse of Communism*, p. 65.
2. Longworth, p. 285.
3. Smith, p. 93.
4. Ibid., p. 95.
5. Ibid., p. 58
6. Ibid., p. 33.
7. Sakwa, p. 425.
8. Ibid., p. 425.
9. Ibid., p. 431.
10. Marples, *Rise*, p. 21.
11. Patrick Cockburn. "Ten Seconds that Shook the World." *Independent*, December 15, 2000.
12. Alfred Friendly Jr. "Chernobyl Revisited: The Nuclear Disaster and Its Aftermath." *Chicago Tribune*, May 30, 1993, p. 7.
13. Marples, *Collapse of Soviet*, p. 21.
14. Ibid., p. 21.
15. Ibid., p. 21.
16. Ibid., p. 23.
17. Watson, *Collapse of Communism*, p. 9.

18. Ibid., p. 22.

19. Ibid., p. 23.

CHAPTER 7

1. Smith, *Fall of Soviet*, p. 19.

2. Watson, *Collapse of Communism*, p. 13.

3. Longworth, p. 289.

4. Ibid., p. 293.

5. Watson, *Collapse of Communism*, p. 13.

6. Marples, *Collapse of Soviet*, p. 44.

7. Smith, *Fall of Soviet*, p. 89.

8. Marples, *Collapse of Soviet*, p. 42.

9. Ibid., p. 42.

CHAPTER 8

1. Marples, *Collapse of Soviet*, p. 121.

2. Ibid., p. 120.

3. Watson, *Collapse of Communism*, p. 80.

4. Smith, *Fall of Soviet*, p. 62.

5. Ibid., p. 95.

6. Ibid., p. 96.

7. Ibid., p. 97.

8. Sakwa, *Rise*, p. 472.

9. Smith, *Fall of Soviet*, p. 100.

10. Ibid., p. 100.

11. Ibid., p. 102.

12. Sakwa, *Rise*, p. 485.

13. Ibid., p. 483.

14. Smith, *Fall of Soviet*, p. 105.

15. Serge Schmemann. "The Fall of Gorbachev/A Special Report: A Russian Is Swept Aside By the Forces He Released." *New York Times*, December 15, 1991.

CHAPTER 9

1. Longworth, p. 299.

2. Todd Brewster. "The End of an Empire." *Life*, January 1992.

3. Ibid.

4. Schmemann, "The Fall of Gorbachev."

5. Jeffrey Sachs. "Helping Russia: Goodwill is Not Enough." *The Economist*, December 21, 1991–January 3, 1992, p. 101.

6. Kevin Fedarko, David Aikman, and John Kohano. "Headache of State." *Time*, April 4, 1994. http://www.time.com/time/magazine/article10,9171,980432=1,00.html.

7. Bill Powell. "The End of an Era." *Newsweek*, January 10, 2000.

8. Adi Ignatius, "A Tsar is Born: Time's Person of the Year 2007." *Time*, December 4, 2007. http://www.time.com/time/specials/2007/printout/0,29239,1690753_1690757_1690766,00.html.

BIBLIOGRAPHY

Alexander II. "The Emancipation Manifesto." In *Russia*, ed. Derek Maus. New York: Greenhaven Press, 2003.

Billington, James H. "The Russian Enlightenment." In *Russia*, ed. Derek Maus. New York: Greenhaven Press, 2003.

Brewster, Todd. "The End of an Empire." *Life*, January 1992.

Churchill, Winston. "The Sinews of Peace." March 5, 1946. Available online. URL: http://www.hpol.org/churchill/.

Cockburn, Patrick. "Ten Seconds that Shook the World." *Independent*, December 15, 2000.

de Hartog, Leo. "Russia Under the 'Mongol Yoke." In *Russia*, ed. Derek Maus. New York: Greenhaven Press, 2003.

Friendly, Alfred, Jr. "Chernobyl Revisited: The Nuclear Disaster and Its Aftermath." *Chicago Tribune*, May 30, 1993.

Gorbachev, Mikhail. Resignation Speech. December 25, 1991. Available online. URL: http://www.publicpurpose.com/lib-gorb911225.htm.

Hosking, Geoffrey. "The Two Revolutions of 1917." In *Russia*, ed. Derek Maus. New York: Greenhaven Press, 2003.

Ignatius, Adi. "A Tsar is Born: Time's Person of the Year 2007." *Time*, December 4, 2007. Available online. URL: http://www.time.com/time/specials/2007/printout/0,29239,1690753_1690757_1690766,00.html.

Knight, Amy. "Joseph Stalin." MSN Encarta Encyclopedia. 2008. Available online. URL: http://www.encarta.msn.com/text_761559200_0/Stalin.html.

Koslow, Jules. "Ivan the Terrible and His Oprichnina," In *Russia*, ed. Derek Maus. New York: Greenhaven Press, 2003.

Longworth, Philip. *Russia: The Once and Future Empire from Pre-History to Putin*. New York: St. Martin's Press, 2005.

Marples, David R. *The Collapse of the Soviet Union: 1981–1991*. New York: Pearson Longman, 2004.

Marx, Karl, and Friedrich Engels. *The Communist Manifesto*. 1848.

Maus, Derek, ed. *Russia*. New York: Greenhaven Press, 2003.

Mawdsley, Evan. "Why the Bolsheviks Won the Russian Civil War." In *Russia*, ed. Derek Maus. New York: Greenhaven Press, 2003.

Mirsky, D.S. "Peter the Great's Governmental Reforms." In *Russia*, ed. Derek Maus. New York: Greenhaven Press, 2003.

Powell, Bill. "The End of an Era." *Newsweek*, January 10, 2000.

Reagan, Ronald. "Remarks at the Brandenburg Gate." June 12, 1987. Available online. URL: http://www.reaganfoundation. org/pdf/Remarks_on_East_West_RElations_at_Bradenburg% 20Gate_061287.pdf.

Sachs, Jeffrey. "Helping Russia: Goodwill Is Not Enough." *Economist*, December 21, 1991–January 3, 1992.

Sakwa, Richard. *The Rise and Fall of the Soviet Union: 1917–1991*. New York: Routledge, 1999.

Schmemann, Serge. "The Fall of Gorbachev/A Special Report: A Russian Is Swept Aside By the Forces He Released." *New York Times*, December 15, 1991.

Sinyavsky, Andrei. "The Effects of the Stalinist Terror." In *Russia*, ed. Derek Maus. New York: Greenhaven Press, 2003.

Smith, Jeremy. *The Fall of Soviet Communism: 1985–1991*. New York: Palgrave Macmillan, 2005.

"Warsaw Pact, The." Modern History Sourcebook. Fordham University. Available online. URL: http://www.fordham.edu/ halsall/mod/1955warsawpact.html.

Watson, William E. *The Collapse of Communism in the Soviet Union*. Westport, Conn.: Greenwood Press, 1998.

Wolfe, Thomas W. "How Stalin's Actions Helped Start the Cold War." In *Russia*, ed. Derek Maus. New York: Greenhaven Press, 2003.

FURTHER RESOURCES

BOOKS

Langley, Andrew. *The Collapse of the Soviet Union: The End of an Empire*. Mankato, Minn.: Compass Point Books, 2006.

Strayer, Robert. *Why Did the Soviet Union Collapse? Understanding Historical Change*. New York: M.E. Sharpe, 1998.

Usitalo, Steven, and William Bennet Whisenhunt. *Russian and Soviet History: From the Time of Troubles to the Collapse of the Soviet Union*. Lanham, Md.: Rowman and Littlefield, 2008.

WEB SITES

The Causes and Consequences of the Fall of the Soviet Union, Center for Global Change and Governance, Rutgers University http://newarkwww.rutgers.edu/guides/glo-sov.html.

The Collapse of the Soviet Union: 10 Years On, BBC News http://news.bbc.co.uk/hi/english/static/in_depth/europe/2001/collapse_of_ussr/default.stm

The Fall of the Soviet Union. The Cold War Museum Web site http://www.coldwar.org/articles/90s/fall_of_the_soviet_union.asp

PICTURE CREDITS

INDEX

ABOUT THE AUTHOR

SUSAN MUADDI DARRAJ is an associate professor of English at Harford Community College in Bel Air, Maryland. She is also senior editor of the *Baltimore Review*, and has written several titles for Chelsea House.